GW00730128

Selected Rock Climbs in
BELGIUM AND LUXEMBOURG

A busy weekend at Freyr, how many climbers can you count?

Selected Rock Climbs in
BELGIUM AND LUXEMBOURG

by
CHRIS CRAGGS

With maps, diagrams and cartoons by Nigel Baker

CICERONE PRESS
MILNTHORPE, CUMBRIA, ENGLAND

© Chris Craggs 1994
ISBN 1 85284 155 9
A catalogue record for this book is available from the British Library

ACKNOWLEDGEMENTS

There are a number of people without whose help this project would not have reached fruition. I would like to thank Nigel Baker whose artwork has added a touch of class to this guidebook and whose incredible enthusiasm, through some difficult times over the past twenty odd years, has always been an inspiration.

I would like to thank all the people who have climbed with me in Belgium and Luxembourg since my first visit in the early seventies: Pete Ackroyd, Pat Shore, Graham Parkes, Pete O'Donovan, Andy Nicholson, Colin Binks, Jim Rubery, Dave Spencer, Andy Watts, Steve Webster, and any one else I have forgotten.

Thanks to all the Belgians climbers who have always made us welcome, especially Serge Massart and "Bene".

Also to Dave Gregory and Steve Webster for proofreading the text and Jean Hulley for checking my pidgin French in the route names. Special thanks to Dave Farrant who was always willing and able to bail me out when the computer was being recalcitrant.

Finally to my "other half" Sherri Davy who has given me much needed support both on the rock and at the keyboard over the three years this project has taken, thank you.

Advice to Readers

Readers are advised that whilst every effort is taken by the author to ensure the accuracy of this guidebook, changes can occur which may affect the contents. It is advisable to check locally on transport, accommodation, shops etc but even rights-of-way can be altered and, more especially overseas, paths can be eradicated by landslip, forest fires or changes of ownership.

The publisher would welcome notes of any such changes

Front cover: **Catching the evening sun, Nigel Baker follows the main pitch of Le Zig-zag, 5+ (HVS 5b), on the upper walls of L'AL LEGNE. He is loving it!**

CONTENTS

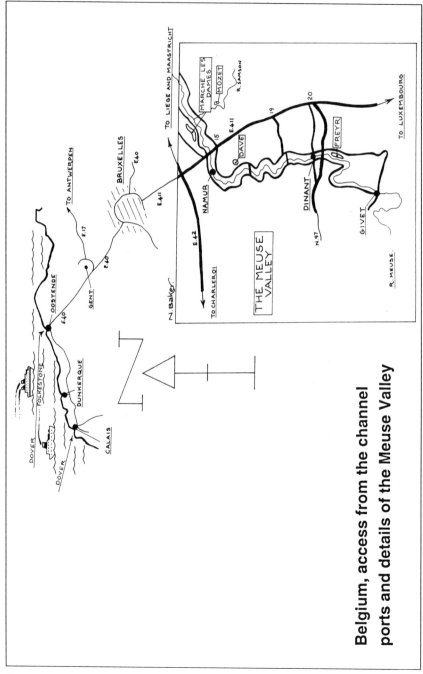

Belgium, access from the channel ports and details of the Meuse Valley

INTRODUCTION

In 1980 Pete Livesey dropped a bombshell in the lap of the British climbing community in the form of a little cardboard-backed book entitled *French Rock Climbs*. Like many others I bought a copy, headed off down the Autoroute du Soleil and was suitably stunned by great cliffs in beautiful settings, being able to climb in shorts at Easter, and the instant attractions of sport climbing. Over the following years the book was much maligned because of the rather stiff grades used in it and because it contained a considerable number of inaccuracies, mainly due to being compiled over an extended period and through a number of visits. With hindsight it is plain to see that at least some of the gripes were from other climbers when they began to discover what they had been missing out on: a climbing paradise that if not quite on the doorstep, was only 24 hours away.

Nowadays the attractions of climbing in southern France are well known and well publicised: Cimai, Ceuse, good old Buoux, the incomparable Verdon, the list is almost endless and new "super-crags" are discovered with almost predictable regularity. But (there is always a but) there are problems. Theft is a common occurrence, it is a bit of a trek for a week, or even a fortnight's climbing, the weather can be VERY hot throughout the summer months, and lastly if you can't climb at least E5 6b (French 7a) you had better stick to Stanage. Now while the former points are certainly true the latter one is very much an impression given by the climbing press. It has to be admitted that in recent years some of the smaller cliffs in the south have been developed with a selection of lower and middle grade routes but these are often crowded, tend to polish quickly, and of course it is still hot for a great part of the year. Is there an alternative? Just possibly.

In Belgium and Luxembourg there is a set of cliffs that have all the attributes of their southern counterparts: perfect rock, plentiful fixed protection and sublime settings (though some are rather urban) and they have a few extra advantages. The northerly position and southerly aspect of much of the rock means that climbing is possible from early spring well through into late autumn without it ever getting too hot, there are routes of all grades and perhaps most importantly the cliffs are only two to five hours from the channel ports. Another bonus is that the Belgian people are exceptionally friendly and most speak at least some English. The open reception we have always received makes a nice change from the dour greeting British climbers often get in some parts of France. In Belgium the locals have long memories and the role that the allies played in these parts throughout World War II has not been forgotten. In contrast there is another nation (naming no names) that is still not made welcome, especially in Belgium; where else in Europe can you pull up at a popular cliff (or beach) and not find a long line of camper wagons already installed, that makes a nice change as well.

I began making flying visits to Freyr in the early seventies on the way to and from the Alps or the "deep south" and have invariably been impressed by the quality of the climbing. In recent years a series of extended visits to the area have reinforced these feelings. Often when asked if they have climbed in Belgium, people's normal reply is either,

"Its flat isn't it?"

or

"No but there is only Freyr and that is supposed to be very polished, isn't it?"

I would be the first to admit that many of the great classics put up originally as aid lines 40 or 50 years ago are manifestly glassy, but then again there are hundreds of more recent climbs that have not suffered this fate, and apart from that have you climbed at Avon, Stoney or Malham recently?

WHEN TO GO

The climbing season in the near continent is longer and more predictable than in the UK. The rather more southerly position and the greater land mass between the cliffs and the Atlantic means that rainfall is much reduced when compared to home. Added to this is the fact that none of the cliffs are intimately associated with high hills so the eternal hissing rain of Wales and the Lake District is largely absent. As recently as Easter 1993 I climbed every day over a two week visit while friends who stayed at home described the weather as "unsettled" to "appalling" depending where in the UK they tried to climb. Winter visits can be repaid with clear warm days climbing on dry rock and with bitterly cold nights, though this is chancy. If you want real winter sun the Mediterranean is a much safer bet. The normally accepted climbing season in Belgium and Luxembourg usually extends from Easter through to October.

FERRIES

For availaility, reservation and brochures:

Dover to Calais, Ostend & Zeebrugge.
   P & O 0304 203388
   Stena Sealink. 0233 647047

Felixstowe to Zeebrugge
   P & O 0304 203388

Hull to Zeebrugge & Rotterdam
   North Sea Ferries 0482 77177

CAMPING AND OTHER ACCOMMODATION

Villatoile Park de Vacances (campsite)
Pont-a Lesse
5500 Dinant Tel. 010 32 82 22 22 85

Village Vacance de Waulsort (cabins)
Monsieur Erik Peterson
Village Vacances
Sur le Pairy 1
5540 Waulsort
Tel. 010 32 82 64 57 61

Camping Bon Repos
39 Rue de Consdorf
Berdorf,
Luxembourg.
Tel 010 352 79631

Camping Belle-Vue
Bedorf,
Luxembourg.
Tel. 010 352 79635

CLIMBING SHOPS

The nearest climbing shop to the main cliffs is at Dave just to the south of the cliff of the same name. The shop is quite well hidden but the location is well signed. At the right turn (when driving north) into Dave, locate and and follow signs for **Setek**. Prices are generally on a par with back home.

CLIMBING WALLS

Belgium has a well developed network of climbing walls some of which are built on an impressive scale and including at least seven walls in Brussels. Prices are on a par with UK walls.

The most convenient wall for climbers based at or near Freyr is the new one at Doische:

Altitude Sport. Rue de l'Emprunt, Doische. Tel. 010 82 67 85 58.
This is close to Givet, 20km south of Freyr. To reach it follow the west bank of the river southwards and at the outskirts of Givet (just short of the French border) bear right up the hill. At the top of this (3 km) turn right and follow the road for 2 kilometres to a left turn into the village of Doische. Guess which building houses the climbing wall!

Summer openings from 2pm to midnight weekdays and 10am to midnight weekends. Winter openings are reduced times and the wall is closed on Mondays. There is also a small inexpensive refuge here.

TOURIST OFFICES

The Belgian Tourist Office
Premier House
2 Gayton Road
Harrow Middx HA1 2XU
Tel. 081 861 3300

Dinant Tourist Office
Rue Grande 37
Dinant
Belgium
Tel. 010 32 82 22 28 70

The Luxembourg Tourist Office
37-37 Piccadilly
London W1V 9PA
Tel. 071 434 2800

Namur Tourist Office
Square de l'Europe Unie
Namur
Belgium
Tel. 010 32 81 22 28 59.2

THE GUIDEBOOK

This volume attempts to describe the routes on a selection of foreign cliffs in a very British fashion. I have given a descriptive account of all of the routes, a star rating to give an indication of overall quality, technical grades for individual pitches, and an "E" grade for routes up to 6c+. I have also included the Belgian grade for comparison. The diagrams are designed to help locate the routes and the photographs are intended to give a feel for the various cliffs and hopefully to inspire you.

The chunky size of the book (A5) has mainly been dictated by the amount of information it contains, and also in the interests of clarity of the diagrams. The vast majority of the climbs in the text are half rope length affairs to lower off and so there is no great need for the guide to be pocket sized.

For the longer routes a small sketch adapted from the description (and carried in your sock?) should be adequate.

THE CLIMBING

All of the cliffs described in Belgium are of high quality limestone, whereas those in Luxembourg are made of excellent hard sandstone. The limestone tends to be pockety whereas the sandstone is covered in ripples and crinkles, on both rock types strong fingers are a great asset. As is the norm on the continent the vast majority of the routes are well protected by substantial bolt runners placed at frequent intervals. On the majority of climbs up to 25 metres in length there are lowering points in the form of fixed karabiners or steel rings at the top of the climbing, allowing for a rapid descent back to the ground. If a route has sections of climbing that are markedly easier than the crux section then the bolts tend to be rather more sportingly spaced. As an example a climb with a 6a crux section may well feel rather run-out on the 5a territory but you can invariably afford to press on in hope as holds and protection will continue to appear when most needed.

All of the cliffs described face "southish" and so are in the sun for a goodly part of the day. Depending upon conditions you can choose to soak up the sun or hunt out the shade depending on season, temperature and temperament. All that is required for the routes described, unless otherwise stated, is a rope and ten or so quick draws. If you feel the need carrying a couple of screw-gate karabiners is a good idea for the bolts on the belays or the crux sections of routes.

The symbol ◊ indicates that a climb or individual pitch is equipped for lowering off using a standard 50 metre rope. For routes without this symbol you will either need to top out and walk down or use double ropes to abseil back to the base of the cliff.

NOTE: *For newcomers to sport routes, a word of advice might not go amiss. The lowering points on many of these climbs consist of substantial stainless steel rings that protrude from "solid rock" in a very comforting fashion. These are often* exactly 22.5 or 25 metres from the ground and there is not necessarily anything that might be regarded as a stance at the belay point. If you are new to sports routes it is worth working out a simple system with your second for getting back down and stripping the climb (before you leave the ground!). Perhaps the simplest set-up is thus:

If more that one person intends to lead the route lower off either twinned (with one reversed) quick-draws or a screw-gate karabiner, and pull the ropes down. If the rest of the team intend to second the route (or once everyone has led the climb) the leader may as well thread the belay rings while he is up there. Clip into the ring and sit on it. Tie an overhand knot in the rope 3 feet from your waist and clip it back to your harness with a screw-gate. Untie your climbing knot from the rope, thread the ring and retie. Unclip and untie the knot in the screw-gate, and you are ready to be lowered back to the ground. This system reduces confusion in that there is no need for the second **ever** to remove his belay plate, and if you drop the rope whilst threading it you are still attached! Also in the unlikely event of a total disaster you are still tied to the rope, clipped through the runners and belayed at all times. Often the belay bolts are offset, when top roping off them it is sensible to equalise the load onto both bolts.

As mentioned earlier some of the older classics are very polished. Modern footwear and liberal application of chalk help to offset this as does a touch of subtlety of technique. I have used the symbol (P) to pick out the more extreme examples of the climbs that have suffered "death by popularity". The star rating takes the state of polish of the climbs into account. I am not suggesting that such climbs be avoided but a little forewarning should prepare you for a skating session, on many of these climbs the quality continues to shine through.

The grading system in most of Belgium is ostensibly the same as the one used in France though in fact the grades here tend to be rather tougher than over the border, especially in the VS to E2 area. For example I have come across 5+ routes that vary from HVS 5b to E4 5c in grade! To avoid giving newcomers to the area too demoralising a shock I have included UK grades (in brackets) for routes up to French 7a wherever this information is available. Feel free to ignore or amend these grades.

The cliffs in Belgium are described first, starting with Freyr and working out from this Mecca. After this the climbing in Luxembourg is described. Enjoy your visit.

READ THIS

Many of the cliffs in Belgium have been bought by the Belgian Alpine Club. They now maintain the footpaths, keep the places tidy and most importantly pay for and install the thousands of bolts that make the climbing here so safe and such a pleasure. They ask people who climb here to respect the cliffs and be a member of their own national mountaineering club. You may be asked for your card so if you are not in an affiliated climbing club perhaps now is the time to support the BMC by joining.

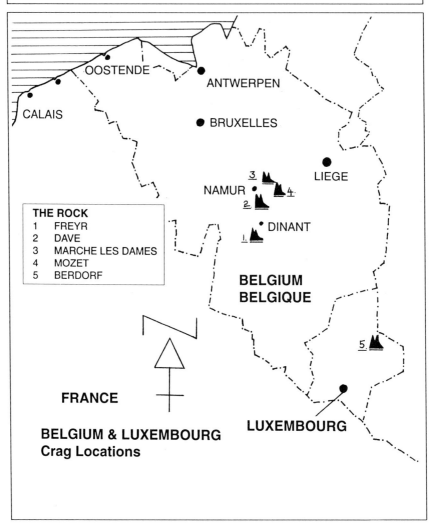

THE ROCK
1   FREYR
2   DAVE
3   MARCHE LES DAMES
4   MOZET
5   BERDORF

OOSTENDE

ANTWERPEN

CALAIS

BRUXELLES

LIEGE

NAMUR

DINANT

BELGIUM
BELGIQUE

FRANCE

N

LUXEMBOURG

**BELGIUM & LUXEMBOURG
Crag Locations**

BELGIUM AND LUXEMBOURG CRAG FACT FILE

The following compendium of information should aid you in deciding where to aim your attentions bearing in mind such inponderables as the abilities of the party and the prevailing weather conditions.

Crags (alphabetically) *less than or equal to*	4	5	6a	6b	6c	7a	7b	7c	8a or above	Total	Faces	Comments
					GRADE SPREAD							
Al Legne	3	12	9	6	6	9	5	3	6	59	W	long classics + hard routes on 'stripy wall'
Berdorf	19	17	18	11	2	6	5	1	1	80	S&W	magic setting
Cinq Anes	2	7	7	2	0	5	0	0	0	23	W	cracks & grooves
Dave	19	27	10	9	4	6	1	2	0	78	W	dry in rain
Jeunesse	6	10	11	1	1	0	0	0	0	29	S	dry in rain
Lion	1	2	2	3	1	1	1	0	1	12	S	polished classics and hard classics
Louis Philippe	2	7	7	4	4	4	0	1	1	30	S	often quiet, steep
Marche les Dames	18	51	7	10	2	1	1	0	0	90	S	mid-grade sport
Mérinos (N)	0	0	0	0	0	1	1	3	1	6	N	steep and hard
Mérinos (S)	14	4	7	3	0	0	0	0	0	28	S	slabby, long
Mozet	12	11	7	5	3	2	1	0	0	41	S	quiet cliff, some loose sections
Pape	0	0	7	8	3	2	0	0	0	20	S	long classics and short harder routes
Totals	96	148	92	62	26	37	15	10	10	496		

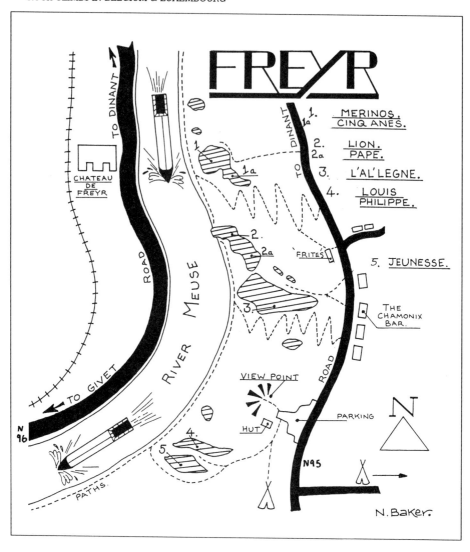

BELGIUM

FREYR

INTRODUCTION

Freyr is not a single cliff but a collection of buttresses and towers rising majestically above a sinuous curve of the River Meuse. It is far and away the most important area in this guide and is well worth an extended visit, or even several extended visits. The crags are up to 400 feet high and the rock is almost invariably impeccable. A road (complete with chip vans and a cafe) runs along the top of the cliffs and bases of almost all the routes are reached by descending well made and well kept footpaths. Some of the climbs on the upper walls are reached by abseil from above; with these a little care is required to make sure you are in the right place. Sacks or trainers can be carried on the longer climbs but if you have a high level of pain resistance it is possible to descend in rock boots, dip your feet in the river to cool them down and then do the climbs in an uncluttered fashion. Another possibility is to descend for the day with butties etc. to climb some of the shorter routes at river level, then finish of up one of the longer easier classics carrying sacks, all very alpine. In recent years there has been a substantial rebolting programme and many of the old pegs and bolts have been replaced by superb large-eyed epoxied bolts. This trend is still continuing. A few routes still sport twinned golos (very small friction fit bolts with square heads) these offer gripping leads as they were never designed to hold leader falls though fortunately these are few and far between (the routes not the bolts). Although not essential it is probably a good idea to carry a light rack (Rocks #4-9) until you get the feel of the place, and double ropes are quite a sensible idea on the longer routes unless you are confident in your ability. The cliffs tend to be very popular at weekends with large number of Dutch and Danish climbers arriving to supplement the local population. At most other times the cliffs tend to be quiet. Spending an evening high on walls of the L'Al Legne as the rock radiates heat and the sun sets behind the Château de Freyr is a magical experience not to be missed.

HOW TO GET THERE

Either take the ferry to Calais ($1^{1}/_{4}$ hours) then follow the rather tedious coastal road to Dunkerque before following the toll free A25 (E42) motorway to Lille and then the Belgian border. Continue on the E42 past Mons, Charleroi and Namur, c.260

km (160 miles) and then follow the E411 motorway south for 35 km (22 miles) to the turn off for Dinant. About 3 hours from the ferry.

An alternative worth considering is to take the ferry to Ostend (4 hours but the same cost as the Calais crossing and a great cruise on a good day) then follow the E40 motorway past Ghent and around the north side of Brussels. Continue down the E411 past Namur to the turn off for Dinant, 200km (125 miles), 2½ hours from the ferry. The cheapest crossings are usually very early morning ones.

Other options such as ferries from Harwich and Hull to ports in Holland or Belgium are also worth looking into if you live anywhere north of the Wash and don't enjoy driving in the south-east of England. The North Sea Ferries from Hull and the P & O from Felixstowe overnight crossing to Zeebrugge is a great way of arriving fresh and raring to go at the cliffs, and although these alternatives initially appear rather pricey the greatly reduced driving distances can make them economically viable.

From Dinant follow the road southwards alongside the river (east bank) in the direction of Beauriang, past an impressive pinnacle, across a bridge and up a long hill. Just over the crest of the hill are a series of cafes on the left and adequate parking on the right. You are now above the cliffs and a short walk out to the look-out point (see map) should make you realise why you came.

WHERE TO STAY

There is a spacious and free but rather Spartan site in the field above the southern end of the cliffs for holders of any national alpine club card (membership of a club affiliated to the BMC is acceptable) but there are no toilets or water at the field. There is a tap and toilets across the road at the Café Chamonix, but you will be expected to make use of more than just these facilities! Recently camping has been allowed behind the cafe, enquire within! There is large and well equipped campsite at Villatoile, 2km to the east of Freyr. This is most easily reached by turning up the valley of the River Lesse by the bridge about 1km before the foot of the long hill described above. Alternatively continue past the cliffs for 200m and follow the narrow road (signed Villatoile) steeply downhill to the campsite. The site is very popular in the high season but there is usually space and there are several alternatives a little further afield if it does happen to be full. Another possibility is to hire a chalet, there are several "Ville de Vacance" complexes hidden in the woods along the banks of the River Meuse and they offer reasonably priced dwellings in pleasant settings. Prices start at about £35 per person per week. Either contact the Belgian Tourist Office at Premier House, 2 Gayton Road, Harrow, Middx, HA1 2XU Tel. 081 861 3300 or call in at the Dinant Tourist Office which is on the corner of a small square (fountains) on the main street. The staff speak good English and are very helpful.

There are many good and moderately priced restaurants and supermarkets in Dinant, and if you happen to be into barbecuing the meat counters are especially worth a visit. Good Belgian bottled beer is inexpensive at the supermarkets, less so in the bars. The Café Chamonix, above the cliff has long been the centre for the local climbers and the owner is very affable. The place offers simple but good food at reasonable prices and very large brandies.

There is an open air swimming pool in Dinant by the river, and another one at a hotel a short distance up the valley from the Villatoile campsite. For rest days there are cruises on the river, show caves, a canoe descent of the Lesse, châteaux to visit and some very pleasant bars.

Each individual cliff has its own character and style of climbing from the delicate face dancing of Le Mérinos, through the soaring groove lines of Les Cinq Ânes, past the great classics of L'Al Legne to the thuggish overhangs of La Jeunesse. All in all there is something for everyone here. The individual cliffs are described from north to south in the following order:

Le Mérinos
Les Cinq Ânes
La Tête du Lion
Le Pape
Al Legne
Louis Philippe
La Jeunesse

The actual approaches to each cliff are given at the appropriate point in the text, and these coupled with the use of the map should ensure that you arrive at the right crag on most occasions. It is worth pointing out that a drive round to the opposite bank of the river is a good way of getting the geography of the various buttresses sorted out.

THE CLIMBING
At the far northern extremity of the cliffs at Freyr there are two small buttresses in the woods just above river level. The most northerly is the **Rocher École** which is a 30ft high wall whilst to the south (right) is the taller (50ft) and more easy angled **Fissures Georget**. Both cliffs have been used for instructional purposes for many years and consequently are very polished. Despite this they are in a pleasant setting and are useful for giving beginners a feel for the sport. They also make a pleasant backdrop to riverside picnics.

LE MÉRINOS

INTRODUCTION

The most northerly of the main cliffs is this massive rambling and generally slabby crag topped by a conspicuous iron cross. Whether the name comes from sheep that used to graze the ledges or the flocks of climbers that are occasionally seen traipsing up some of the easier routes is open to conjecture! The main (south) face is the great grey slabby section of rock, large sections of which appear hopelessly smooth from a distance. This is in fact criss-crossed by an almost bewildering collection of routes and individual pitches, most of which require a delicate touch. Many of the easier routes here have been popular for years and consequently are very polished, I have taken this into account when awarding stars and UK grades. The north face, right under the summit cross offers a number of short, steep and exceptionally tough climbs and the Meuse (west) Face looks out over the river as a mixture of steep walls and slabby grooves.

Note: although the rock at Freyr is generally of impeccable quality loose stones do occur on ledges. The popular and slabby nature of the **Mérinos** means that sitting right under the cliff when people are climbing above is not a good idea, a hard hat is also worth considering.

GEOGRAPHY

The north face is basically a leaning wall 80ft wide and 40ft high set right under the summit of the cliff. The Meuse Face is a triangular section of rock 150 feet high starting at river level and split centrally by a wide low angled ramp running leftwards from a large solitary tree.

The south face is a broad sheet of rock which looks quite featureless from a distance but proves to be much more complicated when you get on it. The most prominent feature of the face is the large ramp, the **Vire de Casserole** that runs down rightwards from the prominent notch in the left crest of the cliff to fizzle out at a series of ledges to the right of the centre of the face, about 100 feet off the ground. Several climbs start from these ledges. Descending diagonally leftwards from here is a thin well travelled break followed by the second pitch of **Les Hermétiques**. The slabby section of rock below this, and above the base of the cliff has some fine routes whilst to its right an earthy slope is the starting point for some longer low grade climbs that run the full height of the right side of the cliff.

APPROACHES

The north face is reached by a short track that leaves the road a short distance to the east of the gully that the Sentier des Pêcheurs descends (see map). On arriving at the rocky ridge that forms the crest of the cliff walk round the right to shelving ledges below the wall (and above a big drop!) For the rest of the cliff descend the Sentier des Pêcheurs (see map) to river level, it arrives at the foot of the cliff at the junction of the Meuse and south faces.

NORTH FACE
This steeply leaning wall has a collection of short pitches, close to the road, in the shade for most of the day and well bolted. The only slight fly in the ointment is the grade of the routes, if you flash all these you certainly deserve a pat on the back! The pint-size height of the routes linked to their high grades means that these are tough cookies. On the very left edge of the cliff is a tiny wall with a couple of trivial offerings. To the right the wall protrudes and there are three more substantial climbs that finish at a common lowering point above the overhang close to the top of the wall.

Gros Locum 7c 30ft ◊
The left line leads past a particularly vicious mono-doigt to the roof. Move left under it to the lower off.

Tchao Pantin 7b 35ft ◊
The next route often has a tape hanging from the second bolt because it is so hard to clip. With the bolt (or the tape) clipped waltz up the wall then move left to join the previous route.

Sans Foi Ni Lo 7c+ 40ft ◊
The right-hand of the trio has a desperate dynamic sequence as the crux before it trends left to join and finish as for the previous climbs.

The next bolt line right was listed a project called **Shingen** in the last guide, I have not been able to find out if it has been completed yet, any takers?

The highest part of the wall has two sustained and highly technical stamina problems.

Mudra * 8a 40ft ◊
The left-hand line of bolts up the "holdless" rock marks the line of the route, it looks absolute mudra.

Chamonix Bad Night * 7c+ 40ft ◊
The right-hand line is supposed to be technically slightly more reasonable, though at these grades it's all a bit academic.

Un Soir * 7a+ 30ft ◊
The right-hand line on the wall starts from a pedestal and provides the warm-up route of the area.

The next climbs described are somewhat more reasonable. They are located on the

MEUSE FACE

This is set just above river level at the very toe of the cliff. As mentioned in the introduction the central feature of this face is a wide slabby ramp that slants leftwards up the cliff starting at a large solitary tree growing close to the rock. Thirty feet left of this tree is the starting point for L'Ecureuil (it means "squirrel") the first route described in this area:

L'Ecureuil ** 4 (Severe) 290ft P

A long and interesting climb following the crest of the buttress from river level to summit cross. It is well polished though the excellent protection helps to offset this, at least to a degree. The start is unmistakable being well burnished and marked by a line of large bolts.

1. 60ft   3+ (Severe) Climb the wall trending generally rightwards to reach a good stance to the right of the crest of the ridge.

2. 60ft   4- (4a) Climb steeper rock to the left of the crest of the ridge until it begins to ease and another comfortable stance is reached.

3. 120ft 2 (Diff) Continue up the ridge passing a possible belay at 60ft until a good stance is reached at the point where a steepening blocks access to the summit of the buttress.

4. 50ft   4+ (4b) The final tower provides the crux of the climb though it can be avoided by scrambling around to the left. The difficulties are short lived and well protected so there are few excuses for failure. The climb finishes on the top of the tower right by the summit cross from where a short scramble leads back to the ridge. A descent path is located to the east of the buttress (to the right when looking at the river).

The narrow inset slab to the left of the main central ramp is the **Départ Duval 2 (Diff) 50ft P ◊** and it can be used as a pleasant variation start to the next climb. The broad left-trending slabby groove in the centre of the cliff gives one of Freyr's more amenable outings, first climbed in 1930 and carrying the sheen to prove it.

Mérinos ** 3- (V.Diff) 230ft P

1. 50ft Climb the "trough" up the centre of the slab to a belay a comfortable ledges on a substantial cemented ring and other metalwork.

2. 60ft Climb above the stance to bulges then move left and continue to the crest of the buttress and a good stance.

There are a couple of more challenging variations to this pitch if you feel you want to test your mettle.

2a. 60ft   3 (Severe)   Le Petit Pet   P Climb the centre of the slab to a bulge which is passed on the right before trending back left to the stance on the regular route.

2b.110ft   4 (VS 4b)   La Cheminée des Lillois P Start as for the previous variation but trend right to enter the long groove line that bounds the right side of the slab. Follow this with sustained interest and not much friction to a belay on the crest of the ridge.

3.   120ft Continue up the ridge passing a possible stance at 60ft until a good ledge and bolt belay is reached at the point where a steepening blocks access to the summit of the buttress. This final steepening is considerably harder than anything else on the climb so follow the ledge round to the left where an easy ramp (but rather exposed, it is probably worth keeping the rope on for beginners) offers a sneaky way to the cliff top. On arriving at the neck of the buttress turn right to get the summit tick and photographs.

Above the foot of the ramp is a steep diamond-shaped wall with a route up its centre:

L'Incognito * 6a (E2 5b) 90ft ◊
Start by the tree close to the rock and climb to a peg runner in the left edge of a diamond shaped block. Move up and left to the start of the bolts (and a horizontal crack with a trio of ancient rusty pegs) then climb the wall boldly trending slightly rightwards to easier rock. Move up and left then from the final bolt runner trend right past a discreet peg to a final difficult move to reach the twinned lowering bolts on the crest of the wall.

Twenty feet to the right of the tree is a route that starts up a slab and then climbs a section of steeper rock to reach the crest of the buttress:

Déviation Poids Lourds * 6a+ (E2 5c) 90ft
Overweight climbers should take encouragement from the name of the route. Climb the slabby lower section trending left past a bolt in a scoop to reach a steep wall. Up this with difficulty keeping to the left of a narrow black streak to a resting place on a ramp. The final steepening leads to easy angled rock with a belay a little higher on the ridge of **La Familiale**.

The right edge of the Meuse face of the cliff is marked by a slabby groove just to the left of where the vegetation takes over. This is the start of another low grade ancient trade route:

La Familiale * 3+ (Severe) 230ft
A pleasant climb though it is rather scrappy in places.

1.   70ft Climb the left-trending groove to ledges at the foot of a steeper band of rock. Step right and climb the wall before moving left to a stance in the main groove just a little higher.

2.   90ft The vegetated groove above the stance was the original line of ascent though the rib on the left is a lot more pleasant. At its top move over to the right to a belay on a good ledge below steeper rock.

3. 70ft   3+ (4b)   Climb up and left to gain access to the chimney with difficulty then continue more easily to the belay at the top of Pitch 3 of **Mérinos** and finish as for that route.

The crack rising above the right edge of the stance provides a more challenging finish to the climb in the form of the **Fissure en Cinq 5 (HVS 5a)** and this can be linked with the top pitch of **L'Ecureuil** to provide a more sustained finish to **La Familiale.**

To the right the cliff swings round to form the slabby and always popular:

SOUTH FACE
There are over fifty routes here that form a veritable spider's web of pitches criss-crossing the face. I have described a selection of the best (and most popular) climbs and it is worth noting that there is plenty of opportunity for "mixing and matching". Obvious combinations are **Petit Navet, La Marmotte** and **La Fissure de Casserole** at HVS 5a,4c,5a,3b, ******** and three **P**s, or alternatively **L'Engrenage, La Jaunisse, La Gamma** and **Les Anciens Belges E2 6a,5c,5c,5b,5c ******** and one **P**. Other variations spring to mind. All of the stances are equipped with lowering rings so a descent from any point on the cliff is reasonably straightforward.

At the bottom left corner of the face is an overhanging and overgrown bay reached by a short scramble. This is the home of three short, hard and unpopular pitches that are not described here. Right again and up the slope are ledges under the centre of the face that are the starting place for a series of more worthwhile and much more popular routes. The ledges are located about 40ft left of the fall line from a great rectangular block stuck on the face 30ft off the ground. The first three routes start at well hidden twin cemented peg belays at the very left end of the ledge system. The steep drop below here indicates why the pegs are there, use them!

Les Hermétiques ** 6a (E2) 180ft
An interesting two pitch climb that ends up at the lower end of the **Vire de Casserole**. From here either select an appropriate way on or abseil 100ft to the ground.

1. 80ft   5+ (5b) ◊   Trend left from the twin peg belay up a flake then continue in the same line to enter a right facing corner. Climb this past a narrow overhang then move up a slippery ramp on the right to an unlikely move that allows a swing into an easy groove. Up this to good ledges.

2. 80ft   6a (5c) P   Follow the obvious break out to the right. There are good holds but they are well spaced and well glossed. At the end of the traverse when all appears lost a long swing down to the right avoids the final blank section. A belay is located just above.

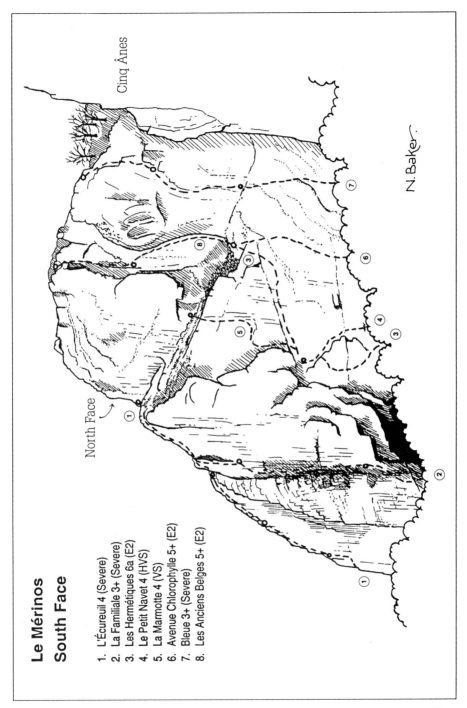

Le Mérinos
South Face

1. L'Écureuil 4 (Severe)
2. La Familiale 3+ (Severe)
3. Les Hermétiques 6a (E2)
4. Le Petit Navet 4 (HVS)
5. La Marmotte 4 (VS)
6. Avenue Chlorophylle 5+ (E2)
7. Bleue 3+ (Severe)
8. Les Anciens Belges 5+ (E2)

North Face

Cinq Ânes

N. Baker

Inner Limits ** 5+ (E2 5b) 90ft ◊

A devious little pitch but with some excellent climbing on it. Those short in stature might dispute the technical grade.

From the twin peg belay move left up a flake (as for the previous climb) then head up the thin slab to the right of the corner (big new bolts next to the old skinny ones) to the overlap that runs across the slab. Pull over this then teeter up the slippery ramp rightwards to its end where a long reach gains a good hidden jug on the arête. Swing back left to a large flake/hole and finish direct to good ledges.

The direct route on this section of slab provides a technical well protected exercise with thin climbing on small sharp edges, more like slate than slate:

L'Engrenage ** 6b (E2 6a) 80ft ◊

From the two peg belay climb straight up the slab past an odd collection of bolts until thin moves gain the overlap. Cross this awkwardly then follow a thin crack past a bendy peg to an easy groove. Continue up this to ledges.

In the centre of the wall is a left slanting groove, access to which is guarded by a line of bulges. Crossing these is the original route of this section of wall, its name does not refer to small Irish workmen but actually means "the little turnip":

Le Petit Navet * 4 (HVS 5a) 80ft P ◊

Above the bulge are two prominent bolts. Reach these by long reaches between excellent but slippery jugs then follow the ramp to the ledges in the centre of the wall. Perhaps the most polished route on this cliff and worth doing just to see how polished limestone can get.

Above the ledges and lower off points for the last three routes is a steep wall with two pitches that provide worthwhile ways on. They both lead to the **Vire de Casserole,** from where there are three options:

   i   follow the ramp left to the cliff top.

   ii   scramble down to the base of the ramp and make a 100ft abseil to the ground.

   iii select a suitable route to the cliff top.

La Jaunisse * 6a (E2 5c) 80ft

From a stance at the right end of the ledges above the previous climbs gain the prominent left trending ramp on the wall above by climbing a steep groove. Follow the ramp to its end and climb steeply to the ledges above.

La Marmotte ** 4 (VS 4c) 70ft P

Start up the steep groove of La Jaunisse but follow ledges out right for 15ft until it is possible to climb straight up on good holds to ledges.

Back at the base of the cliff the next feature rightwards is a huge oblong block with no visible means of support, suspended 30ft up the rock face. The left side of this is climbed by the first pitch of a rather arduous undertaking;

Super-Vol-au-Vent * **6a+ (E2) 270ft** (including 30ft of ledge)
The star is for the third pitch though the rest of the climb has its moments.

1. 70ft 5 (5a) Climb up to the block and follow the corner that bounds its left side (looking at the block, laybacking is probably best avoided). Continue on the same line to a stance 15ft below the break that runs across the cliff.

2. 60ft A0 Cross the break and climb the short bolt ladder (legitimate pulling on the bolts, now there's a refreshing change) up the smooth wall to reach a belay on the ledges of the **Vire de Casserole.**

Descend 30ft rightwards to a belay below an open chimney to the right of a line of overhangs.

3. 80ft 6a+ (5c) Climb the slippery chimney for 15ft then escape out left to less polished rock in a bay. Move left out of this and traverse left to a thin crack with a collection of pegs and bolts spattered about it. Up this until it is possible to move right to a good stance on ledge.

4. 60ft 6a+ (6a) Climb the easy groove above the stance until it is possible to get out onto the buttress on the right. Up this with thin moves around a bulge to reach the cliff top and a well earned tick.

The next route climbs over the centre of the hanging block (or up the prominent white scar if the block has finally given up the ghost).

Full Metal Plaquettes * **6b+ (E3 6a) 130ft** ◊
The hardest route on this section of rock. Start at the name painted on the rock in red and climb to and over the block overhang as quickly as possible to gain the wall above. The bolts in the block may be runners, though on the other hand they may be holding the block on! Continue up the steepening wall rightwards, it being both sustained and technical until things begin to ease. Either lower off the last bolt (possible with a 50m rope) or continue to ledges above and abseil.

Avenue Chlorophylle * **5+ (E2 6a) 120ft**
Start at the name painted in large but discreet green lettering. A polished boulder problem start gains the second bolt and then easier climbing leads to ledges. The crux involves a couple of sketchy moves to leave these and gain a good hole (mud filled after wet weather) following easier climbing past a white area to ledges. Either lower off the last bolt (possible with a 50m) rope or continue to ledges above at the foot of the **Vire de Casserole** and abseil from here.

Up the slope a short way a prominent left-facing and curving flake crack which is the start for two climbs that would be great beginners' routes if their common first 20ft was not so hard.

25

Primus * 4 (VS 5a) 80ft P ◊

Climb the slippery and strenuous flake crack to its top then after a breather move left 5ft to reach and follow a right trending ramp line (about V.Diff) that is followed on good holds to ledges from where a short ascent reaches lowering anchors.

Radius * 4 (VS 5a) 80ft P ◊

Climb the flake as for the previous route (still a battle) then follow a flaky ramp up and right until it fizzles out, then climb the short section of bulging rock to join the previous climb and follow it to the belays.

A little further up the bank from the left-facing flake that marks the start of the previous two routes there is a prominent solitary tree. Starting directly behind this is a route for budding body builders.

Le Beefsteak ** 3+ (Hard Severe) 170ft

1. 70ft   3+ (4b)   ◊ Climb past a square 'feature' at ten feet then continue steeply to join the top of the ramp of Radius. Up this much more easily to its stance.

2. 50ft   3 (Severe) Climb a short left trending ramp then follow the line of bolts directly above the stance on good holds heading for an overhang above. Continue in this line as far as the top of a flake then move right along this to a stance.

3. 50ft Trend diagonally right to another ledge then climb easily up a left trending groove to the cliff top.

Bleue ** 3+ (Severe) 170ft P

Another worthwhile climb at a lowly grade, on good rock and with fine positions. The route was originally protected by blue bolts, hence the name, though these have now been replaced with more substantial boring grey ones. The right edge of the wall is a corner and just left of this is a flake.

1. 70ft   3+ (4a) Climb the flake to its end then continue up a bulging slab to a stance on good ledges.

2. 50ft   3+ (4a) Climb to an overlap and move left under it to an open groove which is followed to a steep exit to the second stance of the previous route.

3. 50ft Trend diagonally right to another ledge then climb easily up a left-trending groove to the cliff top (as for **Le Beefsteak).**

The final climb that starts from the foot of the cliff is an excellent introductory route for beginners having good holds and excellent stances; harder variations are available if required:

Le Cubitus *** 2 (V.Diff) 180ft P

Start at the very top of the slope at the base of the cliff at a cleaned corner.

1. 70ft   Climb the corner to well-scoured ledges which are followed out left for 10ft. From here climb straight up the slab on good holds to the commodious stance of the previous climb.

2. 80ft   Trend right up flaky rock then head back left passing an optional stance until it is possible to move up right to a better stance.

3. 30ft   Climb easily up a left-trending groove to the cliff top.

The final selection pitches described on the Mérinos start from the lower end of the ramp of the **Vire de Casserole**. As mentioned in the introduction these are best used as extensions to routes below although they can easily be reached from the cliff top by abseil or by following the ramp under the north face and then carefully descending the Vire de Casserole to where it fizzles out more or less in the centre of the cliff.

At the bottom end of the ramp is a cave/tunnel. All the routes described are located to the right of this though there are some tough pitches through the bulges to its left. Just right of the cave is a shallow chimney running straight up the cliff face with a steep and polished wall safeguarding access to it. This is

La Fissure de la Casserole * 4 (VS 5a) 120ft P

1. 70ft4 (5a) ◊   The wall directly below the chimney is steep slippery and technical, fortunately it has several well cemented peg runners. Once entered the chimney proves to be much more straightforward and soon leads to good stance on ledges.

2. 50ft   3 (3b)   Move left along the ledge onto the front of the buttress, cross a small bulge and follow the straightforward groove to the cliff top.

The slab to the left of the chimney is home to an excellent and delicate route:

La Gamma ** 6a (E2 5c) 80ft ◊

Climb the initial 15ft of **La Fissure de la Casserole** (to the third peg) then move left into a niche. Pull leftwards out of this and teeter leftwards up a ramp to a new bolt "in the middle of nowhere" (the thin crack of pitch three of **Super-Vol-au-Vent** should be visible 10ft further left). At this point you might want to re-check the comment in the front of the guide about the spacing of bolts on difficult ground. Take a deep breath and press on up gradually improving holds to a big pocket from where easier climbing leads to the ledges.

Immediately to the right of the chimney of **La Fissure de la Casserole** is an impressively smooth slab tackled by two excellent pitches. Both start below bulging rock under the centre of the slab.

Pégase ** 6a (E2 5c) 80ft ◊

Climb straight up steeply but on generally good holds to the second bolt then move left to gain the start of left-hand bolt line (originally this was gained from a short distance up the chimney on the left). Follow a set of deep cracks in the slab until

27

they disappear then make thinner moves to ledges and a giant ring peg. Lower off this (and top rope the next route?) or move left to bigger ledges and alternative lower offs.

Wanted Gratton ** 6b (E3 6a) 80ft ◊

Climb the initial bulges as for Pegase then trend right to the line of big bolts running up the slab. This is followed by superbly thin and sustained face climbing (E4 6b if you don't like slabs?) to the big ring peg at the top. Intense.

Les Anciens Belges ** 5+ (E2) 150ft P

The fine corner that bounds the right side of the slab taken by the previous two routes is a great classic that would deserve three stars (and only E1) if it was not so polished.

1. 80ft 5+ (5b)   Enter the corner from directly below and follow it by laybacking, bridging and finger jamming past a host of cemented pegs and using footholds that will "keep you on your toes". When the difficulties ease trend left to a stance below a rounded water-worn groove.

2. 70ft 5+ (5c)   Climb to the bulge and pass it with difficulty, the two finger undercut in its lip being of material assistance. Once past this obstacle continue more easily by fine sustained climbing to the cliff top.

Les Pierres Tombées ** 5 (HVS) 120ft

The last route on this section of cliff starts from a bolt belay at the lowest point of the Vire de Casserole, the ledge is very narrow here so care is required.

1. 80ft 5 (5a)   From the belay climb the wall trending rightwards to enter a groove that runs up to a large overhang. Climb to this and pull over its right edge before slanting back left to a good stance.

2. 40ft 4 (4c)   Climb the wall trending right to the cliff top.

Spot the newcomer to 'sport-climbing'

N. Baker

LES CINQ ÂNES

INTRODUCTION

A fine crag, 200 feet tall at its highest point, basically taking the form of a massive open corner and with a great set of powerful lines. All the worthwhile pitches have benefitted from the recent rebolting programme though if you don't like "pressing on in hope" up steep rock it may be worth carrying a small selection of medium to large Rocks. From the top of the cliff either descend to the left (facing the river) to pick up the approach path or make one long abseil (or, with a 50m rope, two short ones) down the buttress at the right side of the cliff from massive rings in an outcrop above the top pitch of La Faucille. Other abseil lines are possible but often the anchors are set well back from the cliff top increasing the possibility of the rope jamming.

GEOGRAPHY

The left side of the cliff is a high tower with a couple of worthwhile climbs and to the right of this is the central corner of the cliff. The left arête of the corner is followed in part by the classic Les Cinq Ânes whilst the left wall of the large corner has a curious twisting groove line running up it; Le Tour du Cochon. To the right of the central corner are a whole series of superb crack and groove lines all of which offer well worthwhile routes. The right side of the cliff is steeper and more massive, it is home to a couple of mega-classic routes.

APPROACHES

The cliff is located on the right three quarters of the way down the Sentier des Pêcheurs (see map). Several minor tracks break right from the path and take short cuts to the right side of the cliff. The routes are described from left to right.

The left edge of the cliff is formed by a steep tower of rather unstable looking black and white rock. Below the right side of this is an open shallow groove running straight up the cliff. The first two routes start up this.

Au Balcon d'un Ciné Majestic *** 5+ (E1 5b) 80ft ◊

An excellent pitch offering fine sustained face climbing set at not too extreme an angle. Start up the open groove but trend away leftwards to a lowering point just below a totty looking bulge: delectably delicate.

La Cancan *** 6a (E2) 170ft ◊

1. 80ft 6a (5c) ◊ Climb straight up the shallow groove until it begins to steepen and a couple of moves have to be made using "mono doigts" (fortunately they are pretty good mono-doigts) to gain better holds and a little higher a small stance. Lower off or:

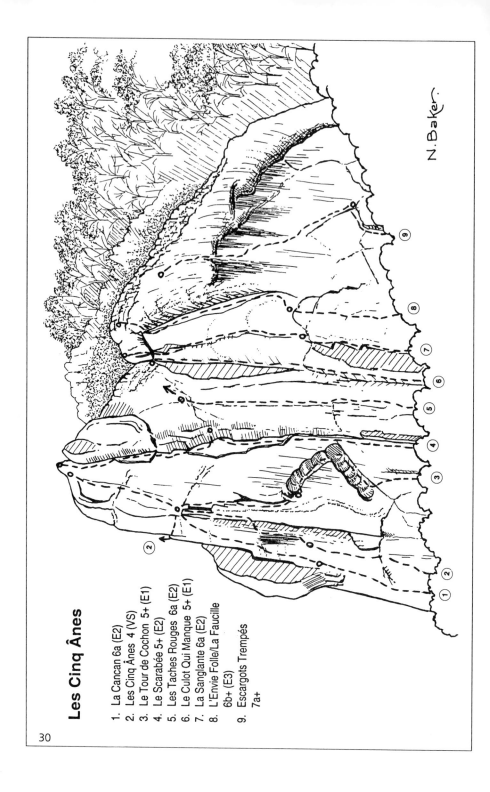

Les Cinq Ânes

1. La Cancan 6a (E2)
2. Les Cinq Ânes 4 (VS)
3. Le Tour de Cochon 5+ (E1)
4. Le Scarabée 5+ (E2)
5. Les Taches Rouges 6a (E2)
6. Le Culot Qui Manque 5+ (E1)
7. La Sanglante 6a (E2)
8. L'Envie Folle/La Faucille
   6b+ (E3)
9. Escargots Trempés
   7a+

N. Baker.

2. 90ft 6a (5b) ◊ Step right and climb straight up the sustained wall and over a rather sinister bulge to a lowering point at the end of the exposed traverse on pitch three of the next climb. Use this or head for the cliff top.

Les Cinq Ânes via La Traversée Bourgeoise *** 4 (VS) 240ft P

A majestic outing with outrageous positions yet at a remarkably amenable grade. Start at the toe of the buttress to the left of the impressive central arête of the cliff where an easy ridge leads up to a series of intimidating black bulges. The whole route is well polished so if in doubt about which way to go follow the glazed rock.

1. 80ft 4- (4b) From the foot of the buttress scramble rightwards and then follow steeper rock on generous holds to a corner. Up this to a belay and small stance.

2. 90ft 4 (4b) Trend right up the steep wall more steeply on even more generous holds (one or two of which feel a bit fragile) until a short traverse right gains the arête in a dramatic position. It is possible to belay here but what a gripper! From here deep cracks are followed on superb rock to another small stance and no apparent way on.

3. 70ft 3+ (4b) Traverse left across the steep and very exposed wall on mostly good holds until it is possible to escape from the drop by swinging round the arête. Scramble easily to the cliff top.

**3a. 70ft 6a+ (E2 5c) La Fissure des Cinq Ânes ** ** The "true finish" is the fine crack in the smooth wall on the right side of the final arête, great climbing, stunning positions and with the crux right at the top. Carrying a couple of wires might be a good idea as the bolts are quite well spaced.

The soaring arête to the right of the start of **Les Cinq Ânes** has three grooves set in its lower section. The left-hand of these is the most prominent and amenable and is recognised by being yellow with black-streaked rock in its angle. This is:

Pulpious ** 4+ (VS 4c) 80ft ◊

The corner offers a short but pleasantly sustained route in its own right or an excellent variation start to **Les Cinq Ânes,** you choose.

The very crest of the arête has two grooves that fizzle out twenty feet above the ground. The left one is white and provides the start of a route with some highly dramatic situations:

La Thérèse ** 6a+ (E2 5c) 90ft ◊

Gain the white groove in the crest of the pillar by climbing a short bulging wall from a flake, first right then left and follow it delicately to a small resting ledge on the right. When suitably refreshed traverse left on to the exposed arête and climb it with difficulty (hint: try crossing hands at the start). Continue up the arête, dramatic but rather artificial, or step left to easy ground, to reach lowering anchors at the point where **Les Cinq Ânes** steps out onto the edge (50m rope required). A logical combination is to continue up the second pitch of **Les Cinq Ânes** and finish by **La Fissure des Cinq Ânes** (see above) to the cliff top thus providing a three-star outing that follows the arête throughout.

The right-hand of the trio of grooves is grey and is the start of a hard route, the upper part of which does not appear to have been rebolted. This lower section is still worthwhile either as a quick tick or an alternative start to the previous climb.

La Sylvia * 6a (E2 5c) 60ft ◊

Scramble onto a flake and climb the steep wall right and then left (as for the previous climb) then press on up the sustained and interesting groove to bolts in the foot of the steep wall above. Lower off.

The rest of the climb is **7b, 6c**. It trends right up "blank" rock to reach the stance at the top of the first pitch of **Le Tour de Cochon**, see below. The final massive pitch climbs the centre of the smooth wall directly above this stance, starting with a short traverse to the right. It looks tough and sadly is only protected by twinned golos at present.

The characteristic water worn tube in the smooth left wall of the main corner is climbed by a rather bizarre but engaging route both in name and execution:

Le Tour de Cochon *** 5+ (E1) 190ft with one point of aid.

A long establish classic, offering excellent sustained climbing. The use of one point of aid appears to make good sense, though the route can be free climbed by the technically gifted. Start at the base of a slab below the soaring central corner of the cliff.

1. 90ft 5+ (5b) ◊ Climb the straightforward slab for 20ft then step left to gain the base of the long flake crack that leads into the base of the tube. Follow the tube first right and then back left with one short sling for aid on an old golo at the change in direction. Getting out of the sling is the crux of the route, though the move can be free climbed (rumour has it) at 6b+. It looks like English 6c in that there is a very large gap in the usable holds. A good stance is soon reached at the top of the tube.

2. 100ft 5+ (5b) Follow a series of awkward cracks in the left edge of the wall past the second stance on Les Cinq Ânes then step back right and follow a continuation crack that runs diagonally rightwards across the smooth face until it is possible to climb direct to the cliff top. The crux is the final couple of moves set in a superb situation, classic.

The main angle of the cliff is followed by:

Climbers on two of the CINQ ÂNES great classics, Les Cinq Anes, 4 (VS 4b), on the left and Les Taches Rouges, 6a (E2 5c), on the right

Le Pino-Prati ** 5 (HVS) 140ft

A pleasant route steep and quite intimidating but not technically too hard.

1. 100ft 5 (5a) ◊   Follow the shallow corner just right of the main groove (or do it direct with floral accompaniment) to a possible constricted stance on top of a pointed block. Continue directly up the corner passing the frowning overhang by laybacking, jamming and wide bridging to reach a stance on the right at the point where the combination corner begins to look a too bit fierce.

2. 40ft   Climb easily off rightwards or have a go at:

Le Scarabée *** 5+ (E2) 180ft

This powerful piece of climbing continues up the impressive leaning corner where the previous route sneaks off to the right.

1. 100ft 5 (5a) ◊   As for Le Pino-Prati without looking up at the true objective of the trip.

2. 80ft   5+ (5b)   Step back to the left and storm the corner by butch laybacking and jamming, without much in the way of resting places or footholds. This pitch used to require a selection of nuts and Friends plus the power to stop and place them. Thanks to the CAB it has been rebolted and such extreme measures are no longer needed. Nowadays the route can be enjoyed to the full.

The wall to the right of the big corner system is seamed by a series of superb crack and groove lines. They are all worth doing. To the right of the twin starts to the big corner is a pair of parallel thin cracks. The left one is **Piranhas * 5+ (E1 5b) 40ft** ◊, short route that leads to the small resting ledge on the next climb. It can also be used as a variation start to that route in which case the overall trip is worth ***.

Les Taches Rouges *** 6a (E2 5c) 120ft

A superb sustained crack line, with a rather slippery crux foothold that has the habit of spitting people off. The name means "the red spots" referring to the original very spaced bolt protection the route used.

Climb the right-hand continuous crack line without deviation, via a small resting ledge (or a stance for the very harassed) to large ledges near the top of the cliff. Magnificent. Abseil descent or scramble off to the right.

In the centre of this section of the cliff is a superb deep groove line: **Le Culot Qui Manque**. Starting up this and breaking out left is

La Galère ** 5+ (E1 5b) 130ft

Start up the main groove and follow it for 50ft until it is possible to step left into

---

Climbers on the third pitch of the classic Les Tourtereaux, 6a (E3 6a)
LE PAPE, one of the most renowned routes in the area

Light and shade on Les Taches Rouges, 6a (E2 5c)

a shallower groove system in its left wall. This gives steep sustained climbing until it fizzles out and it is possible to escape out left to the belays at the top of **Les Taches Rouges**. Abseil descent or scramble off to the right.

Le Culot Qui Manque *** 5+ (E1 5b) 150ft

The centre of the wall contains this fine continuous groove line that snakes its way up the full height of the cliff in a most alluring fashion. Carry a few large Rocks or small Friends if you are feeling at all intimidated.

Enter the groove and climb it steeply (quite slippery and with a pushy feel) until the angle drops back a little and a small ledge is reached on the right (possible belay). Step back into the corner and follow it throughout to the cliff top, superb. The parallel nature of much of the crack in the back of the groove suggests that it must have been a right swine to protect before fixed protection was installed.

To the right of the long groove of the previous climb is another shallower groove with a prominent overhang at the very top of the cliff. The wall to the left of this groove is climbed by

Le Parapluie ** 6a (E2 5c) 150ft

Start 8ft right of the foot of **Le Culot Qui Manque** and climb the steep cracked wall on big holds trending right then back left. Continue up the very crest of the pillar until eventually forced into **La Sanglante** about 10ft below its final overhang. Struggle round this (crux) to finish, a big, big pitch.

La Sanglante *** 6a (E2) 150ft

The right-hand of the continuous groove lines is capped by an obvious overhang. It gives a great climb with the crux just where you don't want it! The climb can be done in one huge pitch though it is usual to split it on a comfortable ledge at half height.

1. 70ft 6a (5c) ◊ From a slab climb into the groove and follow it by sustained climbing until it is possible to exit right to a small stance and welcome rest.

2. 80ft 6a+ (5c) Step back left and follow the groove to the intimidating overhang which is passed with difficulty on the left, at which point the aptness of the name; literally "bloody" becomes all too apparent. A suitable climax to a distinguished route.

The flat front of the buttress to the right of the groove is the starting place for a great combination of pitches:

L'Envie Folle/La Faucille *** 6b+ (E3) 150ft

A logical hook up provides a classical way up the cliff. There are some conspicuous and enticing flakes above a smoother section of rock on the nose of the buttress. Start below these at a bolt belay on a slippery slab.

1. 80ft   6a+ (6a) ◊ Gain the base of the flakes by a short fingery sequence and then romp on using a continually surprising set of holds to good ledges in the centre of the face. There are four generations of belay points on this stance, award yourself five bonus points if you can identify them all in chronological order.

2. 70ft   6b+ (5c)   Gain and follow the superb left-trending layback flake on the right until it fizzles out at a poor resting place under an improbable set of bulges. Swing right and climb through the bulges on good but rather spaced holds.

For purists who prefer to get the full tick, the first pitch of **La Faucille ** 7a+** ◊ is the thin crack in the smooth wall to the right of the initial pitch described above, gained by a traverse from the left, and the top pitch of **L'Envie Folle * 6a (E2 5c)** is the pillar to the left of the layback flake, joining and finishing as for **La Sanglante**.

The right side of **Les Cinq Ânes** is an impressive wall, slabby in its lower half and becoming steeper and more impressive as it rises. There are several hard climbs here, two of which are major classics.

Le Pilier Cromwell *** 7a 150ft
Start up an easy left-facing flake crack and break out onto the wall on its left after 20ft. Follow the vague line of weakness, always trending left if in doubt, eventually to gain the impressive hanging rib to the right of the layback crack of the previous route. Up this on good but spaced holds to the top, 13 clips and what a cracker.

Escargots Trempés *** 7a+ 140ft ◊
1. 40ft   Start as for **Le Pilier Cromwell** and climb the straightforward flake crack to a belay on its flat top.

2. 100ft 7a+   Climb up to a diagonal flake and follow it out left then continue in the same line up a ramp towards the centre of the face to reach a compact white wall. Up this then move left before attacking the bulges that cap this section of wall. On the left above these is a lowering point that allows a yo-yo back to the stance (50m ropes only) or top out.

The white rib that links the lower section of **Le Pilier Cromwell** with the upper section of **Escargots Trempés** is **Gastropodes Hallucinogènes ** 7a+ 140ft ◊**.

Limaçon Defoncé * 7a 130ft ◊
From the stance onto the flake (as for **Escargots Trempés**) climb straight up the wall for 50ft to a series of bulges. Move right under these to gain a deep hole then traverse left below the final set of overhangs until it is possible to climb straight up to a lowering point (50m rope only).

LA TÊTE DU LION

INTRODUCTION

A relatively small crag being only 150 feet high at its centre, set right down by the waterside and composed of perfect though occasionally highly polished rock. The logic behind the name of the cliff is most apparent when seen from the View Point or from the opposite bank of the river, with the rock's resemblance to a sedate reclining lion complete with shaggy mane being quite extraordinary. All the climbs apart from the crux section of the original way up the cliff, **La Tête Du Lion**, are on the sunny south face.

All of the routes described here finish on the crest of the cliff which is a knife edged ridge. From this airy crest an abseil is the easiest form of descent, either back down the line of the climb or from the col at the lowest point on the ridge, see below.

GEOGRAPHY

The cliff is basically a flat wall, slabby on the right and steeper away to the left and bounded on the far left by a blocky ridge. All of the left side of the cliff rises directly from a narrow riverside path which is often under water nowadays. No routes are described starting from this path for the obvious reason that 7c+ with wet boots is nobody's idea of fun. A couple of climbs that start away on the left and traverse in above the tide line are included and are ideal for devotees of Gogarth and Swanage

The right side of the steepest section of cliff is marked by the steep groove directly above the shore line, this is the first pitch of the classical **Sirène**. Up the slope to the right is a steep polished corner behind some bushes; this is the start of the excellent **R²**. On the right side of the face is the well glossed deep groove followed by **La Grunne**. The main features on the upper section of the right side of the cliff are two fine flake cracks, the left one being the top pitch of **R²** and the right one belonging to **La Focquet**.

APPROACHES

The foot of the cliff can be approached by either walking down the Sentier du Pecheur (see map) and turning left at the bottom to skirt under the foot of the cliff, or by descending the path under **L'Al Legne** and following the riverside path northwards under the **Rocher du Pape** to the foot of the **Lion**.

> NOTE. There is a narrow concrete path along the very foot of the cliff that is used on the approach from the Sentier du Pecheur. Since the building of the flood control dams further down the river this path is often inundated, as are the starts of one or two of the routes. It is usually possible to wade

round but don't stray too far from the rock and also keep an eye out for those occasional big barges that come thundering past.

Descent: for all the routes that finish on the thin crest that forms the top of the cliff, either abseil back down the route or traverse carefully along the cliff top (keeping the rope on?) to the lowest point on the ridge. From here either descend the ten foot wall to the north to reach easy ground then paddle back round or abseil 100ft down the south side of the Lion from cemented pegs. This latter course of action is just possible using a doubled 50m rope but with the ends about 10ft off the ground, leaving a slippery section of down climbing. A modicum of care is required.

The routes are described from left to right.

La Tête du Lion * 5+ (E1 5b) 270ft P

A hoary classic, now showing its age but still worthwhile. It only has a couple of hard moves and these are well protected, perhaps the whole exercise could be used as Alpine training (if you know what I mean, nudge nudge, wink, wink). Start at the left edge of the cliff just above high tide.

1. 40ft   V.Diff.   Step right above the water and climb the easy ridge to a stance and twin peg belays at the point where it begins to steepen up.

2. 90ft   5 (5b)   Climb up to the bulges then move left and round onto the north face where a short steep wall is climbed with difficulty (or peg pulling) trending right until you can regain the crest. Continue more easily to a stance.

3. 120ft   2 (V.Diff.)   Traverse the crest of the ridge clipping into any fixed gear that you pass until you arrive at its low point. Descent as described above.

Le Super Dentier & Trio Fingers ** 6b (E4) 180ft

A couple of routes than can be linked to provide an illogical and rather arduous way up the cliff. Despite the irrational line, the climbing is good and the situations are excellent.

1. 50ft   Solo the first pitch of **La Tête du Lion** to a two peg belay overlooking the water. The rock on this pitch is polished, don't slip!

2. 70ft   6b (6a)   Traverse down and right to reach a large forbidding black bulge which is traversed by strenuous undercutting (not overly protected for a "sport route") to reach easier rock which is climbed to an uncomfortable cramped stance below a steep wall on the right.

3. 70ft   6b (6a)   A steep and sustained pitch protected by rather unusual bolts! Power through the initial bulges trending right then climb straight up until a ledge on the right can be reached. A finish directly over the final bulge is possible though easy ground is very close by to the left, the choice is yours.

La Tête du Lion

1. La Tête du Lion 5+ (E1)
2. Coco Beach 6c (E4)
3. Trio Fingers 6b (E4)
4. La Sirène 6c (E4)
5. La Focquet 6a+ (E2)
6. R² 6a+ (E2)
7. La Puissante Morsure 5+ (HVS)

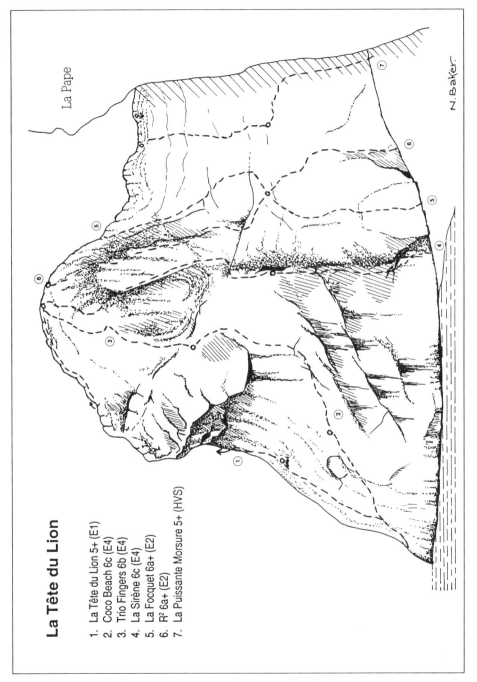

La Pape

N. Baker.

Mash Mallow * 6b (E3)

A worthwhile route with a short strenuous crux and some great situations, not a route for sufferers of hydrophobia.

1. 60ft   3 (Severe) Follow the ridge of **La Tête du Lion** for 15ft then traverse right rising slightly to a small stance 30ft below a large double roof.

2. 60ft   6b (5c)   Traverse horizontally right along a ramp for 15ft then climb steeply to enter the imposing hanging corner above. Up this until it is possible to make a bold swing out right on big holds to gain the front of the buttress. Climb straight up the rib to a small stance.

3. 50ft   4 (4b)   Follow a ramp to the right then climb the slab to arrive at the highest point of the Lion.

Coco Beach * 6c (E4) 210ft

Another trip above the tide line offering fingery climbing on excellent rock. An obvious choice for your first 6c solo as the landing is very forgiving (always assuming you can swim!). Start as for **Mash Mallow**.

1. 60ft   3 (Severe) Follow the ridge of **La Tête du Lion** for 15ft then traverse right rising slightly to a small stance 30ft below a large double roof.

2. 80ft   6c (6a)   Continue along the line of the first pitch by following the disappearing ramp for 30ft. At its end step right and climb a blind crack then swing right again and sprint up a short wall to gain easier rock. Up this to the uncomfortable stance of **Trio Fingers**.

3. 70ft   As abseiling off is not really an option either finish via **Trio Fingers** 6c (6a) making the whole trip worth ******, or follow the ramp leftwards for 15ft and finish easily as for **Mash Mallow**.

The next route described in full is the brilliant **Sirène** which starts from the water's edge under the centre of the cliff (see below). The impressive wall to the left of the first pitch of **Sirène** has two hard routes that are reportedly superb.

God Save the Queen 8a 100ft traverses 20ft left from above the initial wall of **Sirène** then tackles a bevy of bulges before joining the final few moves of **Coco Beach**.

Lâches des Fauves 7b+ 155ft, climbs to the niche 30ft up **Sirène** then moves out left (prominent long sling on a bolt) for 15ft before climbing straight up the wall keeping to the right of **Mash Mallow** and **Trio Fingers**. Splitting the pitch at the **Trio Fingers** stance reduces the grade of the route to 7a+.

La Sirène *** 6c (E4) 150ft

A brilliant climb with a varied combination of pitches, once compared to Stoney Middleton's **Wee Doris** which is a bit like comparing diamonds and coal dust!

Start at the water's edge on the right side of the causeway, the second may want to tie himself to the convenient tree to avoid being dragged to a watery grave

The crux moves at the top of Sirène, 6c (E4 6b), LA TÊTE DU LION. Climber: Colin Binks

if the leader fails to clip the first bolt.

1. 80ft   6b (6a)   From the beach move left and climb into the hanging chimney groove which is followed by strenuous graunching or technical face climbing to its closure at an inverted niche. Make difficult moves rightwards over the roof then continue more easily to a cramped stance in a shallow cave cum recess.

2. 70ft   6c (6b)   Climb straight up until it becomes imperative to move right. Thin moves lead out to a ramp which is followed easily to the final obstacle. The bulge on the right is crossed by a boulder problem sequence, short and sharp, and very safe.

Cocaine Fingers ** 7a 160ft

A sustained and strenuous pitch that scales the impressively smooth rock to the left of the second pitch of **Sirène**.

1. 80ft   6b (6a)   As for **Sirène** to the cramped stance. This should provide a pleasant warm up, though if you find it a touch tough it is perhaps better to continue up **Sirène**.

2. 80ft   7a   Step left onto the wall and climb directly to a bulge which is passed rightwards with difficulty. Continue up the steep sustained wall to another bulge and pull rightwards over this with difficulty (not again) to attain the ramp at the top of the second pitch of **Sirène**. The original finish skirts out left to finish as for **Trio Fingers** though the crux of **Sirène** lies just to the right and is perhaps a more worthy conclusion to a great route.

To the right is a small memorial plaque bolted to the wall, just to the right of this is a route who's name requires care in pronunciation, especially if you are struggling on the climb:

La Focquet ** 6a+ (E2) 140ft P

1. 70ft   6a+ (6a)   Start to the right of the memorial plaque and climb a short wall to ledges then trend right up a smooth ramp (no sneaking round to the left). Step back left and climb a short steep wall to arrive at a small, foot crushing stance.

2. 70ft   6a+ (6a)   Move right to pass the bulges then climb directly up the wall to reach the right-hand of the prominent crack lines. Follow the fine continuous crack line strenuously to the summit.

R² *** 6a+ (E2) 160ft P

A great route with three short but well-protected hard sections. To the left of the deep corner that bounds the right side of the cliff is a short overhanging groove with a series of very polished holes running up it, start here.

1. 80ft   6a+ (6a)   Climb the strenuous corner on painful pockets (the surreptitious use of a metal handhold is most difficult to avoid) then head left

Approaching the end of the first pitch of R², 6a+ (E2 6a), LA TÊTE DU LION, Climber: Chris Craggs

up a series of scoops linked by tricky moves to reach the uncomfortable stance of the previous route.

2. 80ft   6a+ (6a)   Move left and then gain access to the hanging corner via a hard move. The flake above proves to be much more amenable, and despite appearances to the contrary is adequately protected, get romping!

La Puissante Morsure ** 5+ (HVS 5b) 100ft P
An ancient classic with the gloss to prove it. The initial section is particularly slippery though things improve as height is gained. Start in the big corner that bounds the right side of the Lion and climb it to the top of the second scoop. From here traverse to the left onto the open face and a possible stance, then head straight up the wall on a continually surprising set of holds.

La Grune * 4+ (VS 4c) 90ft PP
Could this be the most polished route in the world? The big corner is followed throughout and provides an interesting exercise in zero friction climbing. Fortunately it is possible to bridge past much of the glaze as long as your foot work is up to it, monumental.

The traverse of La Tête du Lion has its own dangers

LE PAPE

INTRODUCTION

A large cliff which has a somewhat English feel about it being both bright white and occasionally a little on the loose side. The original routes of the cliff followed strong natural lines running the full height of the face. More recent offerings are shorter contributions, mainly concentrated around the base of the wall. There is a good selection of climbs here across a range of difficulties, in a pleasant riverside setting making the cliff well worth a visit.

GEOGRAPHY

The cliff is basically a flat fronted square wall, 200 feet high and bounded on the left by the leaning arête and flat roof of **Le Pilier Davaille**. The most conspicuous feature of the left side of the cliff is the black diagonal overhangs followed by **Le Z** whilst to the right of this are the shallow grooves systems taken by the major classic of **Les Tourtereaux**. Right again and roughly in the centre of the cliff is the roofed-in corner followed by the central section of **Le Herman Buhl** and the final feature before the cliff degenerates into a broad grassy gully is another corner system, with a bright white left wall, followed in part by **Le Pape**.

APPROACHES

The cliff is positioned squarely between the diminutive Tête de Lion and the great mass of L'Al Legne. At the point where the Pape runs into the Al Legne is a substantial and long-running archaeological excavation; please stay out of the diggings. The easiest approach is to take the path as for L'Al Legne and walk under its bottom left corner to reach the foot of Le Pape. The base of the cliff can also be reached from the Sentier des Pêcheurs by paddling round or abseiling over La Tête du Lion; see that section for more details if required.

The left edge of the cliff takes the form of an impressive leaning wall, north facing, 120 feet high and capped by a large roof with a crack running through it. This is **Le Pilier Davaille**, a spectacular two pitch A1 that is largely equipped and offers good wet day sport for those who can remember how to aid climb. Quite why this magnificent challenge has not yet been free climbed is a bit of a mystery though the first twenty or so aid points have been by-passed. If things run true to form it will be hailed as the best and hardest route in Belgium about a week after this book arrives in the shops!

To the right of the arête of the cliff is a prominent diagonal black overhang which is followed by **Le Z** (see below). The wall below this is home to several short and worthwhile routes. The rock on the lowest section of this wall is rather poor in places though it improves rapidly with height (always assuming you can do the initial moves). The first two climbs here start at a steep slab at the very edge of the wall.

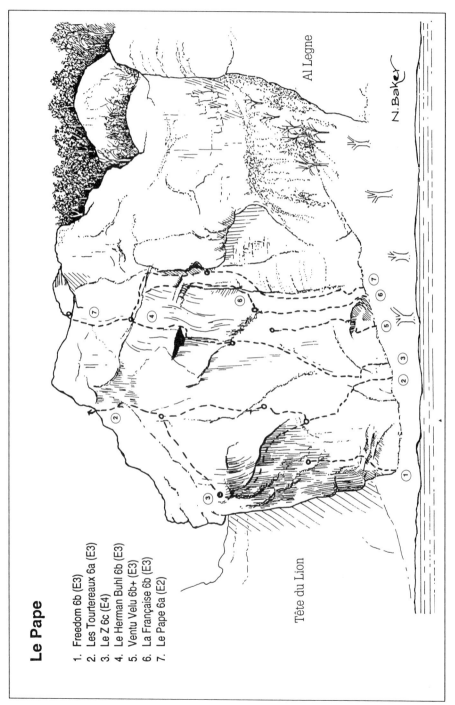

Le Pape

1. Freedom 6b (E3)
2. Les Tourtereaux 6a (E3)
3. Le Z 6c (E4)
4. Le Herman Buhl 6b (E3)
5. Ventu Velu 6b+ (E3)
6. La Française 6b (E3)
7. Le Pape 6a (E2)

Tête du Lion

Al Legne

N.Baker

Approaching the lowering point on Plaisirs Éphémères, 6a (E2 5c), LE PAPE. Climber: Chris Craggs. The overlap taken by Le Z, 6c (E4 6a) is prominent above

Plaisirs Éphémères * 6a (E2 5c) 80ft ◊
Climb the delicate slab to the bulges then make a couple of technical and bold-feeling moves into the yellow left-facing corner above. Climb this to its top then step right and follow a series of easier grooves on rather transient rock to a flake which leads to the lower off. It is possible to continue for a second pitch to join the tail end of the second pitch of **Le Z**. This deserves an extra "E" grade and an extra star.

**Freedom ** 6b (E3 6a) 70ft ◊
Follow the previous route to the first bolt then move right under the bulges using a series of pockets until below the left edge of a shallow blank groove. Swing awkwardly right and enter the groove by a couple of thin moves back up and leftwards, then continue more easily to the lower off and freedom.

To the right the lower section of the wall is gently overhanging; two routes climb through the rather totty initial bulges to reach better rock above.

47

Realité du Zen ** 6c (E4 6a) 70ft ◊

Definitely a route for the masters of levitation; if you think you can do it, then you can do it (probably).

Climb through the initial bulges first left then right to reach some drilled finger holds (subtle or what?) which are used to reach the roof. Pull left round this (crux) to a poor resting place then step back right and follow good holds linked by technical moves to reach the lower off.

Frite Physique ** 7a 70ft ◊

A fine direct line which is easier (or at least possible) for the tall. The right-hand line has a technical start to reach holds below a bulge which is passed by a massive reach off a suspicious finger pocket or a short dyno from the same. Above this follow the awkward rib and groove (either one or a mixture of both) to the belays.

Just around to the right is the rather crowded starting place for a whole collection of excellent routes. Some of their names are painted on the rock to try and ease the confusion, though it is quite easy to end up following the wrong bolt line. The first of these routes begins at the left-hand of a pair of left-facing flakes and is marked by a small blue arrow painted on the rock.

Samarkan *** 6b (E3 6a) 90ft ◊

A great climb, sustained, varied and well protected. It is just possible to lower off the route on a 50m rope. Climb the flake to a white pockety scoop and a little higher a rest on the

The crux moves on Realité du Zen, 6c (E4 6a), LE PAPE. Climber: Chris Craggs

left. Continue in the same line (the left-hand bolt line on this section of wall) by sustained climbing to the foot of a smooth white wall which presents the fingery crux (hint: try swinging in from the right) until easier moves lead to a lower off from the belay bolts at the top of the second pitch of **Les Tourtereaux**.

Starting up the right-hand of the twin flake cracks is;

Les Tourtereaux *** 6a (E3) 270ft

One of the great classics of Freyr, this route was once described as being like **Adjudicator Wall, Robert Brown** and **Dead Banana Crack**, one on top of the other. What a load of drivel, it's much better than that! Although all the pitches are 6a (5c) the first and third ones are longer and much more sustained than the second and fourth. If you want an easy ride make sure your mate kicks off with pitch one.

1. 80ft   6a (5c)   Climb the flake to its top until it is possible to trend left linking a series of generally good holds by tricky moves until it is feasible to swing round the arête and climb up to a small stance.

2. 50ft   6a (5c)   Step up then traverse back round the corner to the right and climb a short steep all on small holds to a good stance in a recess.

3. 80ft   6a (5c)   Step left to enter and follow the steep and pushy groove that runs up the wall to where it fizzles out. Trend slightly left to another good stance below some black overhangs.

4. 60ft   6a (5c)   Behind the stance is a black pockety bulge which is best climbed quickly as the holds are good but the angle is a little excessive. As easier rock arrives swing left to escape from the drop and scramble to a tree belay. Descend to the left to the gap between the Lion and Pape, or head straight through the trees to pick up the Sentier des Pêcheurs, or by two long abseils.

Le Z *** 6c (E4) 300ft

A long route with an excellent and challenging second pitch. Start as for **Les Tourtereaux** at the right-hand of the pair of left-facing flakes. Other more taxing starts are available by using any of the routes to the left.

1. 80ft   6a (5c)   Climb the flake to its top until it is possible to trend left linking a series of generally good holds by tricky moves until it is feasible to swing round the arête and climb up to a small stance.

2. 90ft   6c (6a)   Follow the overlap! This is one pitch where a detailed description is rather superfluous. At the end of the overlap pull into an open groove and belay at its top. From here either abseil off (double ropes required) or:

3. 70ft   5 (5a)   Trend right up the pleasant ramp line to the belay below the black bulges on **Les Tourtereaux**. A classical HVS pitch, pity it is so hard to get at!

4. 60ft   6a (5c)   Behind the stance is a black pockety bulge which is climbed on good finger pockets. Swing right then move left to reach easy ground where easy scrambling leads to a tree belay. Descend to the left to the gap between the Lion and Pape or head through the trees to pick up the Sentier des Pêcheurs, or make two long abseils back to the ground.

To the right of the twin flakes is a steep slab bounded on the right by a diagonal crack line and split by a much thinner crack line which provides the start to:

Belle Isa * 6a (E2 5c) 70ft ◊**
A great little pitch, sustained and delicate offering unlikely moves on excellent rock.
Climb the thin crack (easier than it looks) to ledges below a short steep wall. This wall is the polished crux of **Le Herman Buhl** (see below) so move left onto the open face and follow the bolt line with sustained interest and a touch of delicacy to reach the lower offs.

Le Herman Buhl * 6b (E3) 250ft P
An ancient classic (1957) much used for peg pulling practice in "the golden olden days" which accounts for its glossed nature. There are only two short hard sections and the use of a point of aid on each pitch reduces the overall grade of the route to a "big" E1 5b and increases its star rating to **. Start at the easy right trending crack line.

1. 100ft   6b (6a or 5a with one point of aid**)** Follow the crack to ledges then move left to a large bolt in a polished wall. Free past this (or have a sneaky pull) to reach a right trending flake line which is followed past a possible stance and without any real incidents to a small stance at the foot of the groove line that runs up to a huge black overhang.

2. 90ft   6b (6a or 5b with a point of aid**).** Climb the polished groove to the capping roof and make a couple of improbable moves out right onto the open wall. Up this trending right to reach a belay below an open groove in the final wall; the last pitch of **Le Pape**.

3. 60ft   6a (5c or 5b with one point of aid**).** Climb the short tricky wall to enter the groove then continue up the fine flake system to the cliff top.

To the right of the diagonal crack that **Le Herman Buhl** starts up is a slab with a solitary bolt and above this is a shallow left-facing flake. This is climbed by:

Le Physique Solaire ** 6a (E2 5c) 70ft ◊
Start from a grassy ramp and climb straight up to the base of the flake. Sprint up this to reach the diagonal ramp of **Le Herman Buhl** then cross this to continue in the same line by interesting face climbing to a lower off.

The bolt line that starts from the optional stance on the first pitch of **Le**

Herman Buhl just to the right of the lower off used by **Le Physique Solaire** and runs up the wall above is **Jules de Chez Schmit d'en Face 7a+ 90ft**. It looks very good.

Some distance to the right there is a prominent orange cave reached by a short scramble. Roughly half way between the grassy ramp at the start of **Le Physique Solaire** and the cave there is a solitary bolt line;

Hazewee a Laeken ** 7a+ 210ft
A fine climb, long sustained and tough. The bottom section of the first pitch can be done as a pitch in its own right to a lower off at 80ft. This is **6b (E3 6a) ***
1. 110ft 6c   Climb the initial bulging wall then trend right to a possible lower off. Continue over a bulge and up the rib that bounds the right side of the groove of **Le Herman Buhl** to reach the end of its crux traverse. Pull leftwards over the bulges and belay almost immediately.
2. 60ft 7a+   Climb the wall trending left to reach ledges, where it becomes obvious that the route needs a direct finish. Move right to join and finish as for **Le Pape**.

The next four routes start around the prominent large orange cave a short distance up the cliff. Skirting the left edge of this orifice is;

Boulin Malin ** 6b (E3 6a) 90ft ◊
Climb carefully to the first bolt (or climb into the cave, clip a bolt and step left to it) then make difficult moves up the wall (keep left) until a superb jug comes to hand. From this continue up the sustained but easier wall trending slightly to the right to reach ledges and a lower off.

Ventu Velu ** 6b+ (E3 6a if you can reach the holds, E4 6b if you can't) 90ft ◊
Climb into the left edge if the cave and lean out right to gain the line of pockets (often greasy) that split its lip. A long reach or a one arm pull up! gains better holds, then the steep wall is climbed with the occasional tricky move to reach the lower off of the previous climb.

La Française * 6b (E3) 220ft**
A superb climb the highlight of which is the stunning second pitch. The first pitch can be done as a climb in its own right at **6a (E2 5c) ***
1. 90ft 6a (5c)   Climb the right edge of the cave and make a couple of unlikely moves up the short steep wall to easier ground. Continue to the base of a smooth wall that is passed on well hidden pockets. Continue past a flake to a small stance.
2. 70ft 6b (6a)   Traverse right into the superb corner system and climb it to below the tiered bulges. Pull powerfully through these then continue up the sustained wall to the ledges below the ledges on the third pitch of **Le Pape**.

Either lower off back to the previous stance and abseil from there or traverse left to a belay below the final pitch of **Le Pape** and finish up this **6a (5c) 60ft**.

Running across the smooth white scoop from a short distance up the corner system on the second pitch of **La Française** is a traverse that eventually joins **Le Herman Buhl**. This is **Élégance 6c 80ft**, it looks sustained, technical and quite superb though the definitive guide book only gives it one star.

Le Pape *** 6a (E2) 260ft P

A great classic put up in 1934. The climb is polished but somehow it doesn't seem to matter too much as you follow this trail of history through the heart of the cliff.

1. 130ft 5+ (5b)   Climb the right edge of the cave for 10ft then teeter right along a narrow ledge to climb the short technical and slippery wall to ledges and an optional stance. Move left and climb past a oversize peg before stepping right into a long groove that is followed until it begins to steepen up (**La Française** continues straight up this). Spiral out to the right and climb the rib to a stance in a niche below a continuation groove.

2. 70ft   5 (5a)   Attack the imposing crack (La Fissure Gergovie) with conviction, fortunately it is not as hard as it looks, to reach ledges. Traverse easily left to a stance below the only break in the head wall.

3. 60ft   6a (5c)   Climb the short tricky wall to gain the fine flake system that runs to the cliff top. Before you pull over have one quick glance back down the face: superb.

The pillar to the right of the long groove on the first pitch of **Le Pape** has three routes on rock that is rather less than perfect in places. The generous and substantial bolt protection makes up for this shortcoming. The most prominent feature of this section is a narrow band of overhangs at 30ft. The first two climbs cross this.

Les Couilles du Pape ** 6b (E3 6b) 90ft ◊

The left-hand climb has a fierce technical start using a glued flake to get through the initial bulges (no sneaking round to the right) and gain a ledge. Climb through the bulges above on good but spaced holds to reach a short hanging corner. Up this with a touch of commitment then swing right and continue more easily to a lower off.

Torremolinos ** 6a (E2 5c) 130ft ◊

A massive pitch up the centre of the pillar; take plenty of quick-draws. Climb the initial wall on indifferent rock to a ledge then climb through the bulges on pockets trending first left then right. Continue with sustained interest to the lower off of the previous route but continue past this, up the rib and away to the right to a belay in the Niche du Pape. Abseil back to the ground or lower back to the top of the previous route and abseil from here.

The lower wall of Les Couilles du Pape, 6b (E3 6b). The original classic of the cliff, Le Pape, 6a (E2 5c) climbs the groove above the climber and then continues up the groove on the right.

To the right are some conspicuous large pockets at 20 feet. These are utilised by

Les Pavis du Nord * **6b+ (E3 6a) 70ft** ◊

Climb to the pockets then swing right and climb through the bulges on suspect rock before heading straight up the wall to a lower off where the angle eases.

53

Les Groenlandais ** 6a (E2) 190ft

A good climb with fine positions; it could do with a direct finish to take it all the way to the cliff top.

1. 130ft 6a (5c)   Start at the right side of the wall where a diagonally pockety seam breaks through the bulging wall. Follow the pockets strenuously to reach easier rock. Move left and gain the long open rib which is followed to enter a groove. Up this the cosy stance in the Niche du Pape.

2. 60ft   6a (5b)   ◊Move out right and climb the sustained front of the buttress in dramatic situations until easier moves lead to the top of the tower. Either lower off from here back to the niche and abseil to the ground, or climb down the corner on the left and follow the ledge system out to the left to join and finish up the final pitch of **Le Pape 6a (5c) 110ft**.

Climbing 'classics' does have its advantages

L'AL LEGNE

INTRODUCTION

This is the largest cliff at Freyr, and it contains many of the area's traditional classics, as well as a multitude of much newer fare. The cliff rises over 350ft from the wooded banks of the River Meuse and it is undoubtably the most impressive (and some would argue most important) cliff in this guide. The crag contains well over 100 routes many of which gained classical status a long time ago; they now carry the scars to prove it. The routes vary in grade from Grade 3 (Severe) to at least Belgian 8a+ and in length from less than half a rope, up to six pitches. The rock almost without exception is impeccable, the outlook is sublime and there is something here to suite almost every taste.

This guide makes no attempt to describe all the climbs on the cliff but rather to offer a cross-section of what is available, as an introduction and an appetiser. By the time you have worked through these you should have a good idea of the geography of this magnificent chunk of limestone and can then start to explore some of its more remote corners. The routes that start from the foot of the cliff are described first (from left to right), followed by the climbs that are approached from the cliff top by abseil.

GEOGRAPHY

The cliff is basically a huge wedge-shaped west-facing wall. It is at its highest on the far left where the route **Le Spigolo** starts almost at river level, and it tapers away to the right eventually disappearing into the hillside high up the bank close to the road. To the right of the arête of **Le Spigolo** the lower section of the cliff appears rather scruffy, though on closer acquaintance there are some fine steep walls hidden in the trees before a riser leads up to the rather battered ledges at the foot of the long groove system that runs the full height of the cliff. This is the unmistakable line climbed by **La Directissima**. To the left of the prominent final corner of **La Directissima** is a superb smooth wall hanging in a most dramatic setting, whilst to its right are two other large hanging groove systems. The central one is the final pitch of **L'Échec du Siècle,** and the right-hand one has the great squat tower of **Le Pilastre** at its foot.

Further to the right the upper walls of the cliff consist of largely "unclimbable" sheets of smooth grey rock and below this is the zebra-striped wall that contains many of the area's hardest climbs. The classical and monstrously chiselled **Prises Taillées** cuts through the right edge of this area and then there is a final short wall with some pleasant pitches before the cliff fizzles out into the hillside just short of the road.

The central section of L'AL LEGNE in the evening sun. The climber high on the cliff
on Le Zig-zag 5+ (HVS 5b) is approaching the same position as
the front cover shot.

APPROACHES

There is roadside parking just to the south of the last "Friterie" at the top of the long hill out of Anseramme (see map). A series of paths lead into the wood and on to the top of the cliff less than 100 metres away. Be warned; much of the cliff edge path is very polished and a swallow dive from here would be unlikely to end in the river. Just a short distance further to the south several paths lead into the trees to join the main track that descends the steep bank a short way out from the rock. This path is well made but can be slippery when wet. The heavily-wooded nature of the slope means that the rocks are only glimpsed occasionally through the foliage, though these glimpses are certainly impressive. Eventually the descending path reaches the riverside path almost directly below the terrace at the start of **La Directissima**. Further to the left is a soaring arête that basically forms the left edge of the cliff, this is climbed by:

Le Spigolo 5+ (E1 5b) or 4+ (VS 5a) ** 440ft (P)

The longest vertical route at Freyr, first climbed in 1934, and now showing signs of its venerable age. There are two possible finishes to the climb, a fine direct one or the original way which sneaks off to the left up the last two pitches of **L'Al Legne**. The climb starts a short distance left of the corner of the cliff at a polished pockety wall that leads into the base of a huge open groove.

1. 60ft 4+ (5a)   Skate up the steep lower wall by any one of several lines (in the words of Fagin "you gotta pick a pocket or two") to a belay in the base of the large groove system. A slippery and technical pitch that contains bolts set a comforting distance apart.

2. 110ft 4 (4c)   Follow the groove until it is possible to move out on the fine arête on the right. Continue up this in great positions and on excellent rock to a stance on top of a pillar from where there is a choice about the way on:

For technicians and seekers of a toilsome time,

3. 100ft 5+ (5b)   Trend left up ledges to the foot of a thin crack that is followed with difficulty to a small but comfortable stance below steeper rock.

4. 70ft 5 (5a)   **La Sortie Des Flamands.** Climb rightwards up steep rock and over bulges (don't look down) to gain the crest of the ridge and a selection of belays.

Or for good time charlies and those hopelessly harassed,

3a. 100ft   Trend left as for **3**, but step round the corner where easy ledges are followed up and back round to the right to the small but comfortable stance on the direct route.

4a. 70ft   Slant left and escape around the corner from the snarling exposure to where easy rock leads up the rear of the face and then back to the crest of the ridge where the two ways reunite.

5. 100ft   Scramble along the crest of the ridge, rope optional but advisable, to the cliff top. All very Alpine, and a suitable end to a great climb.

L'Al Legne

1. Le Spigolo 4+ (VS)
2. L'Amour/Lecomte 5+ (E1)
3. L'Hypothénuse 4 (VS)
4. La Directissima 6a (E1)
5. Le Pilastre 6c (E5)
6. L'Échec du Siècle 6c (E4)
7. La Variante Duchesne 5+ (E1)
8. La Grippe Intestinale 6a+ (E4)
9. Les Prises Taillées 6a+ (E3)
10. Le Zig-zag 5+ (HVS)

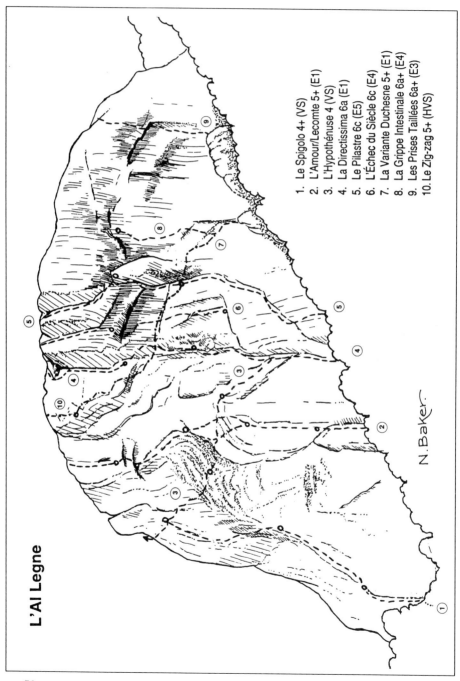

N. Baker.

Down and to the right of the towering ridge of **Le Spigolo** are a series of short clean wall and slanting corners at the foot of the cliff which run out into more vegetated terrain a little higher up.

Warning

This area is directly below the central section of some easier climbs that cross the face on a series of ledges over 150 feet up. Beware of the possibility of stone fall.

There are several short tough climbs here the first of which starts just right of the arête to the right of the start of **Le Spigolo.**

Khumbu 7b ** 40ft ◊

Follow the succession of finger pockets that starts just to the right of a commemorative cross up the steep wall to the edge of an overlap, then trend right to a belay station. A tough pitch though somewhat safer than its glacial namesake.

Les Cinq Soeurs 7a ** 40ft ◊

Climb the centre of the wall to the right of the cross by "sequency" moves until it is possible to trend left to the belay of the previous climb.

The overlap to the right is **La Croisière Fantastique** and the arête just to its right again is **Vive La Femme**, I have been unable to find grades for these.

Around to the right is a steep smooth-looking slab with two lines up it. The left-hand one is

Aragorn * 7c+ 90ft ◊

Climb the completely holdless slab by advanced levitation techniques directly to the left end of the overlap high on the wall, then pull round this to the lower off.

The best route on this section of rock starts at a flake below the left end of a prominent left slanting overlap at 80ft.

Nina Hagen 7a ** 90ft ◊

A fine sustained and varied pitch. Climb the shallow groove then scratch desperately up the steep face trending gradually leftwards until a short traverse to the right gains the groove. Butch your way up to the end of the overlap then pull rightwards over the capping roof to reach the belays just a little higher.

To the right is the point where the diagonal flake followed by the upper part of **Nina Hagen** reaches the ground. Starting here is a weighty little number which would be a pleasant pushover if it wasn't for what the locals describe as a "bloc" move. If you don't know what that means you will soon find out!

Middle Rocky II * 6b (E2 6b) 80ft ◊

Climb up to the overlap and mantelshelf over it awkwardly. Follow the straightforward ramp until a short "blank" wall is reached. Float like a butterfly up this or take a dive and stay down for the count.

Fifille Pieds D'Acier ** 6c (E4 6b) ◊

The smooth wall just to the right is well equipped, well 'ard and well worth doing. Climb the steep lower section, make a brief detour into **Middle Rocky** then step back right and continue up the wall before eventually rejoining **Middle Rocky** a short distance below the lowering point.

L'Amour & La Voie Lecompte *** 5+ (E1) 380ft

A redoubtable combination of varied pitches that offer a superbly sustained way up the face. It should come as no surprise to find that the route is immensely popular, it is worth starting early if you do not want to join a queue.

At the right side of the lower wall of the cliff and 10ft left of a scruffy groove is a prominent and well marked corner containing a small overhang at 50ft.

1. 70ft 5+ (5b) Follow the steep sustained thin crack in the corner past the bulge to reach a good stance on the left with a better one even further left. Probably the hardest pitch on the route so if you find it a bit tough it is worth persevering.

2. 90ft 5+ (5a) A continuation corner extends the theme of the first pitch, offering more sustained climbing, mainly jamming and bridging, until things begin to ease and more straightforward climbing leads up ledges for 20ft to a well pounded stance on **L'Al Legne**. From here there are two choices both of which are worthwhile; the former is more fun, the latter more technical.

3. 80ft 6a+ (5b if you are tall, harder if not) **The Connection.** Climb diagonally right easily then up a short crack until a traverse leads left to the wire cable pendulum point on **L'Hypothénuse**. Free climb leftwards across this after clipping a high bolt (or throw ethics and caution to the wind and swing gleefully across on the cable, always remembering to return it for the next team) then either belay immediately, or, better, climb diagonally to the left for 20ft to a small stance in a groove.

3a.70ft 5+ (5b) **Le Chaînon Manquant.** Perhaps a more logical line. Climb the crack and slab running diagonally left from the stance, following the crack throughout is quite tough so stay low, to reach the left end of the pendulum. Either belay immediately or, better, climb diagonally to the left for twenty feet to a small stance in a groove.

4. 80ft 5+ (5b) Move out right from the stance in the groove and climb the smooth and technical rib past bolt and peg runners heading for the impressive double overhang that hangs over this pitch. Pull leftwards over the first roof on a flake then use undercuts to grope right for the "big daddy" of all

The sustained crack system that forms the second pitch of L'Amour, 5+ (E1 5b), L'AL LEGNE. Climber: Nigel Baker

jugs, if you don't find it first time keep reaching right. Swing gloriously rightwards then continue up and right to a small and exposed stance on the left just a little higher.

5. 60ft 5 (5a) The shallow corner above the stance is bridged past an overhang and then gives steep but easier climbing to the cliff top; a fittingly interesting and well positioned finale to a great expedition.

Pull Marine ** 6a (E2) 160ft
An alternative finish to the final two pitches of **L'Amour & La Voie Lecompte** is a little harder but still well worth doing. It can also be approached via the first three pitches of **L'Hypothénuse**.

1. 100ft 6a (5b) From a belay to the left of the wire pendulum cable (you did free across didn't you?) climb straight up the steep sustained face trending slightly to the left until under the right edge of a large overhang. Move left under this and pull round it on good holds (as for the regular route) to reach a stance a little higher.

2. 60ft 5+ (5c) Climb up a couple of moves then pull out right onto the exposed rib. Climb this direct, easing gradually as height is gained to a final steepening and the cliff top.

La Directissima * 6a (E1 5b) 310ft P**
The most classical of all the classics, a great route up a striking line, first climbed

in 1935. Parts of the route are well polished but the quality continues to shine through. Start by scrambling leftwards to ledges below the open groove that runs up to the left-hand and most prominent of the three large corners that dissect the central section of the upper walls of the cliff.

1. 140ft 4 (4c)   Follow the beckoning groove line over a couple of bulges to a comfortable stance. This pitch can be split if required.

2. 50ft 5 (5b)   Climb up and right to below frowning bulges which are tackled on large but burnished holds until it is possible to shuffle rapidly left into the foot of the upper groove system. Climb this a short distance to a small but well-appointed stance with dramatic views in all directions.

3. 120ft 6a (5b)   Follow the superb sustained corner system past a niche (possible stance) by a variety of bridging, finger-jamming and laybacking moves until it is possible to exit out to the right for maximum exposure. Vintage or what?

Starting as for **La Directissima** are a couple of even more venerable routes that find sneaky ways up the cliff by heading away leftwards and seeking out weaknesses which allow them to reach the upper section of the ridge that forms the left edge of the cliff. Both offer interesting trips at very amenable grades, though on both routes the amount of traversing demands a steady approach by the second man.

L'Al Legne ** 4- (Severe) or 4+ (VS 4c) if the pendulum is done free. **530ft**
The original line of the cliff, first climbed in 1933 by the royal team of Princes Albert and Leopold. The route takes the easiest line up the face, but despite the lowly grade the amount of traversing means the climb is not really suitable for novices. Unfortunately the central section of the climb involves a lot of grazing across grass ledges, though the interesting start and well posititoned finish of the climb make it well worth doing. Start as for **La Directissima**.

1. 70ft   Climb the polished groove until it begins to steepen where it is necessary to keep left. A small ledge is available here for a stance, or alternatively continue up the next pitch.

2. 50ft   A well-marked flake crack leads leftwards out of the groove and is followed on good holds to reach a comfortable stance on a horizontal ledge system.

3. 40ft   Follow descending ledges down to the left past a possible stance to a smooth section of rock (La Banane) with a knotted rope hanging down it. Either free climb across (4c) or treat the route more traditionally and get swinging. A good stance is available just to the left.

4. 100ft   Easy ledges linked by the occasional tricky moves lead horizontally leftwards out to the arête of the cliff at the point where things begin to improve again at a comfortable "sit down type" stance.

5. 100ft Step left and climb the arête on good holds until it is possible to trend back to the right to a belay in an oppressive niche. Is there any way on from here?

6. 70ft Traverse around the corner away from that horrible exposure and climb the north side of the arête, over a small bulge to reach the crest of the cliff.

7. 100ft An easy ridge leads from here to the summit. Do yourself a favour, keep the rope on and clip any fixed gear you pass! A superb ending to a "good romp round".

L'Hypothénuse *** **4 (VS 4b) or 5+(HVS 5b)** if you free climb the pendulum. **440ft**
Another long and interesting route with Pitch 3 an absolute must for cowboys, Tarzans and commandos. Start as for **La Directissima**.

1. & 2.   120ft   Severe As for **L'Al Legne** to the stance on the ledge system. If you are in the right place there should be a wire cable with a piece of piping attached to it, lodged behind a flake visible up to the left.

3. 70ft Climb up and left to a "blank" and well-scoured section of rock, grasp the cable and get running (technicians can free climb across the slab after clipping a high bolt at safe 5b). Once established on the other side return the cable to its resting place for your partner to use then traverse further left to a good stance and belays.

4. 80ft   4 (4b) Continue leftwards at the same level to a shallow chimney/groove which is climbed for 30ft until it is possible to exit to the left to where more traversing leads to a stance in a niche.

5. & 6.   170ft Continue easily to the top as for Pitches 6 & 7 of **L'Al Legne**. On the other hand if you fancy something more challenging, try throwing yourself at the steep and exposed

5a. 70ft   5 (5a)   La Sortie des Flamands Climb rightwards up steep rock and over bulges (don't look down) to gain the crest of the ridge and a selection of belays. Continue easily to the cliff top.

To the right of the lower section of the groove line of **La Directissima** the face juts forward and there is a steep slab of rock split by a diagonal ramp running up right to the base of the great tower of Le Pilastre. The base of this slab consists of a series of narrow grassy ledges, the left side of which are reached by a short scramble from directly below. The right side of the ledges can be reached from a point a little further to the right by passing through the bushes. There are a selection of shorter climbs here that cross the prominent ramp, and also there are the lower pitches of routes that run all the way to the cliff top. All of the routes are described from left to right in relation to their starts, even though some cross each other higher up the face.

Below the lowest point of the diagonal ramp there is an open and well-trampled niche reach by a short 20ft scramble up easy rock. This is the starting point for a number of routes:

Petibull * 6a+ (E3 6a) 70ft ◊

Climb the niche then step left and follow the bolts up a smooth slab to a ledge, then move right to a lower off. A slippery little teaser.

L'Échec du Siècle *** 6c (E4) 300ft

A fine long climb, even though it was once "the failure of the century". The original approach was rather devious (now taken by **Le Dièdre de L'Échec**, see below) though this has now been straightened out to provide a direct approach to the superb climbing up the middle one of the three groove lines visible in the upper part of the cliff.

Start at the broken niche.

1. 70ft ◊ **6a (5c)** Climb the niche then move right to pick up and follow the line of pink bolts up a steep slab to a good stance. This is the upper half of **Chocolat Bleu** (see below). It is perhaps logical to do all of this route **6a (5c)**, so as to earn an extra tick.

2. 120ft 6c (6a) Behind the stance is a line of nice new green bolts. Follow these up the wall and over a bulge to reach a narrow break at the foot of a steeper white wall leading to a prominent niche in the overhangs. This intervening wall is climbed with difficulty on a poor selection of pockets and the occasional undercut. At the roof move left then pull out right and belay immediately in a superb situation.

3. 110ft 6a (6a) Step right and make a couple of slippery moves to gain the undercuts that form the base of the big corner system. Step left and follow the superb sustained groove throughout by finger jamming, bridging and laybacking up the magnificent corner. One of the finest pitches at Freyr.

Le Dièdre de L'Échec ** 5 (HVS 5a) 130ft ◊

The original start to **L'Échec du Siècle** gives a pleasant route in its own right at an amenable grade.

1. 70ft 4+ (4c) From the top of the open niche climb onto the ramp and follow it up to the right without incident for 40ft until it begins to steepen up and a rising line can be taken out to the left to reach a small stance at the foot of a long left-facing groove.

2. 60ft 4+ (5a) Follow the groove with sustained interest over a couple of bulges until it is possible to pull right to a ledge and belays. Abseil from here or follow the **Traversée des Six Jours 5+ (HVS 5b)** and **Le Zig-Zag 5+ (HVS 5b)** to the cliff top for a *** outing. See below for the description.

Superb positions on Les Trois Saurets, 6b+ (E3 6b), L'AL LEGNE

Le Pilastre *** 6c (E5) 300ft

Another long and historical outing, that originally resorted to much aid. As a free route it is both varied and tough. The climb takes the left side of the prominent tower to a world-class stance and then the smooth and sustained right-hand of the three grooves in the head wall. Climbed totally free it is a tough cookie, though the protection bolts are very well placed if it all proves a bit much!

1. 90ft 3+ (Severe) Start in the open niche (left of the pink bolts) and gain the base of the ramp that descends from the foot of the tower. Romp up it to a stance below a bulging corner crack. The first pitches of either **La Claudio 6a (5c)** or **The Wall 6a (5c)** offer less logical but better quality and harder starts; see below.

2. 70ft 5+ (5b) The polished corner is very character building, especially the final offwidth, though on the blunt end it is possible to bridge most of it. The flat top of the tower is an island in the sky, a great spot to lie down and recover from the exertions below and to prepare for what is to come.

3. 50ft 6c (6b) The steep wall behind the stance is climbed diagonally leftwards with great difficulty using tiny and unhelpful holds. A small stance is your reward, or if you thought the wall was easy you may as well press on.

4. 90ft 6b (6a) The groove is remarkably sustained, very slippery and doesn't contain many holds. Thin finger-jamming and laybacking appear to be the best way to make progress, with an occasional rest in a bridging position. Brilliant.

Chocolate Bleu ** 6a (E1 5c) 70ft ◊

Just to the right of the open niche where the previous four routes started is a line of pink (how very fetching) bolts running up the slab. Climb a short discontinuous series of cracks to one very precarious reach to gain access to the ramp. Cross this and climb the continuation wall with a tricky move leftwards into a good pocket. Romp on to the ledges and lower off.

To the right of the line of pink bolts there are two other lines of big new bolts that are close together. The leftmost line is

Keikefred ** 5+ (E1 5b) 120ft ◊

Climb the steep slab until the rock becomes "blank". The old bolt line going out left from here is the neglected route of: **Trottinette 6b 70ft ◊** so make a couple of unlikely blind moves up and right to good holds (the moves feel like **6a** until you do them!). Swing right then continue to the ramp. Follow this for a couple of moves then climb up over ledges and some dubious rock to gain the right arête of the groove followed by **Le Dièdre de L'Échec**. This gives excellent sustained climbing on great holds and with fine positions to a small stance and belays below much steeper rock.

On the final moves of À L'Ombre des Cocotiers, 6a (E2 5c), LE LOUIS-PHILIPPE

Abseil from here or follow the **Traversée des Six Jours 5+ (HVS 5b)** and **Le Zig-Zag 5+ (HVS 5b)** see below to the cliff top for a *** outing.

Le Zygomare ** 5+ (E1 5b) 110ft ◊

The right-hand bolt line gives a pleasant pitch with some good climbing, though it is somewhat disjointed because of the ramp of **Le Pilastre**. Start directly below the steep corner that bounds the left side of the tower of Le Pilastre.

Climb slightly leftwards up a discontinuous crack line on good holds to reach the easy ramp on the first pitch of **Le Pilastre**. Step left and continue up another crack system that runs the full length of the continuation slab to ledges and belay bolts. Abseil descent or see the comments at the end of the previous route for an excellent alternative.

La Claudio *** 6b (E3) 350ft

A long diagonal heading leftwards up the cliff. What the route lacks in line it makes up for in positions and climbing. The original final pitch is rarely done and has not been rebolted, so the route is described finishing up the superb final pitch of **L'Échec du Siècle**. Start at a prominent flake to the left of a large spindly tree and 10ft right of the start of **Le Zygomar**

1. 140ft 6a (5c)   Climb the initial flake then move right to where one hard move on a solitary glossy foothold (or a quick snatch) gains the continuation flake. Up this on good holds to ledges then shun the groove on the left and climb the short steepening up the front of the pillar on good holds to a major break and possible belay. Move round to the left and belay a short distance to the left of the big corner groove of **Le Pilastre** pitch 2.

2. 100ft 6a (5b)   Climb the shallow groove in the wall 10ft left of the corner on rough rock to the line of roofs. Traverse delicately leftwards under these until it is possible to pull out right and belay on the stance at the end of pitch 3 on **L'Échec du Siècle**.

3. 110ft 6c (6a)   The groove above is entered with difficulty and followed with sustained interest. It gives a fitting finale to the route; if you have done it before it is well worth doing again.

The Wall *** 6a (E2 5c) 90ft ◊

A fine direct pitch that starts behind a tall thin tree below the right side of the tower of Le Pilastre. It is well protected by a line of big golden-yellow bolts. Climb straight up the wall on excellent rock eventually bearing away left to the stance right below the tower: well worth seeking out.

To the right an awkward blocky scramble leads up and right to the foot of a prominent left-facing flake crack. Belay just to the left of the top of the flake on a solitary bolt. Three worthwhile and varied routes start from here, the first of which is a midgrade mega classic.

La Variante Duchesne, La Traversée de Six Jours and La Variante du Zig-Zag * 5+ (E1 5b) 350ft**
A majestic combination of pitches that form a logical way across the heart of the cliff at a very reasonable grade. The lower section of the first pitch is probably the technical crux though the amount of traversing on the rest of the climb means that a circumspect approach is required by the second man. Perhaps the best route of its grade in Belgium! The latter two thirds of the climb can be enjoyed by starting up any of the routes around the ramp of **Le Pilastre** (see above).

1. 100ft 5+ (5b) La Variante Duchesne ◊ From a bolt belay by the top of the blocks climb the rather slippery flake crack (the odd wire might not go amiss as the bolts are "sportingly" placed, especially the third one) over an overlap until a nicely technical traverse leads out left below the continuation of the overlap. Thin moves between good holds lead eventually to a stance below the front of Le Pilastre.

2. 100ft 5+ (5b) La Traversée de Six Jours Move left and climb the slab to gain the obvious break that leads out towards the arête. Follow this with interest until at the point of maximum exposure it turns tricky. Make a difficult swing down and round the corner to reach the glossy rock on **La Directissima** and follow this awkwardly to a good stance in a niche. The second can stay clipped into the bolt that protects the crux moves until after he has done the moves (thank goodness).

3. 100ft 5+ (5b) La Variante du Zig-Zag Traverse left onto the slab and climb it delicately to a bulge. Pull over this on good holds then step left and climb direct on much more polished pocket holds to a big fat peg. Make an intricate little traverse out left until it is possible to swing into a short groove which is climbed to a small stance on the left. Looking down the pitch is very photogenic, it appears to be totally blank!

4. 50ft 4 (4b) Follow the polished cracks above the stance to the cliff top and the end of a memorable trip.

Going Wild ** 6c (E4 6a) 150ft
Interesting, technical and occasionally blind climbing on superb rock. Start by following **La Variante Duchesne** to just before the end of its traverse and a possible constricted stance on twin ring bolts (or move left to a better stance). Climb rightwards following the line of bolts up magnificently compact rock, pity it doesn't have a few more holds! Eventually a couple of bolder moves gain a groove, below steeper rock. From here trend up and left into the easy groove (possible yoyo) and a little higher a belay on top of Le Pilastre. Finish up this **6c, 6b (E5 6b, 6a) 140ft** or abseil off.

La Grippe Intestinale * 6a+ (E4 6a) 140ft** ◊
A magnificent and spooky route that skirts the left edge of the great striated wall

The long first pitch of La Variante
Duchesne, 5+ (E1 5b)L'AL LEGNE.
Climber: Nigel Baker

that is the main feature of the right side of the cliff. The route was originally protected by spaced, twinned golos, and was a very serious lead. These have been replaced by 10mm bolts but the integrity of the pitch has been preserved, if you know what I mean!

Start at the bolt belay as for **La Variante Duchesne** and climb the slippery flake (if you need wires on this slightly run-out section you had better have a rethink!) and move left to the centre of the traverse. Cross the two set bulges by fingery moves to reach marginally easier angled rock. Continue by sustained climbing trending very slightly leftwards until more difficult moves can be made up and right to reach a resting place at a tiny overlap. Move right into a groove (crux) then layback rapidly to a belay on twinned maillons. Getting back down from here is a little problematical with a single rope; any ideas?

To the right the cliff presents a magnificent streaked wall, capped by a line of bulges that cuts across the cliff, and above this hangs a series of smooth boiler plate slabs. There are at least twenty-five routes on this section of wall with only a couple of offerings at less than 7b, and over a dozen routes of 7c and above. Habitués of the "cat-walk" at Malham Cove could have a happy time here, with great climbing complemented by immaculate sunbathing. Unfortunately the routes generally are far too hard for me and they are also difficult to describe because of the featureless nature of this section of cliff. Rather than ignore these pitches altogether I have taken the liberty

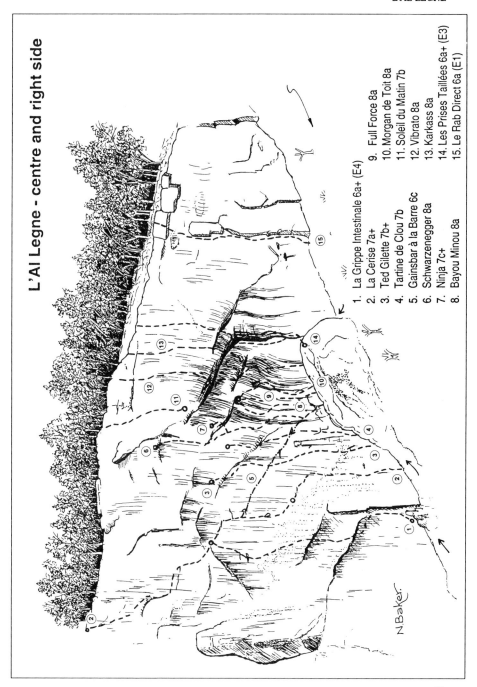

L'Al Legne - centre and right side

1. La Grippe Intestinale 6a+ (E4)
2. La Cerise 7a+
3. Ted Gilette 7b+
4. Tartine de Clou 7b
5. Gainsbar à la Barre 6c
6. Schwarzenegger 8a
7. Ninja 7c+
8. Bayou Minou 8a
9. Full Force 8a
10. Morgan de Toit 8a
11. Soleil du Matin 7b
12. Vibrato 8a
13. Karkass 8a
14. Les Prises Taillées 6a+ (E3)
15. Le Rab Direct 6a (E1)

N.Baker

of taking the grades and star ratings of the best dozen routes from the 1987 Freyr guide and offer a topo-diagam as a starting point for those interested in this superb wall. Any detailed descriptions or amendments to the grades will be gratefully received.

The easiest approach to the crest of the domed buttress below the centre of the wall is via the easy groove that is used to get at **Les Prises Taillées** (see below). The first three of these routes start to the left of the domed buttress and to the right of **La Grippe Intestinale**. From here the top of the buttress can be approached via a tricky scramble (knotted rope in place).

The routes on the diagram of the striped wall are, from left to right:

La Cerise *** 7a,6b,7a+ 320ft
A major diagonal finishing on the superb headwall above **Le Pilastre**.

Ted Gilette ** 7b+ 110ft ◊
A smooth grey wall on razor edges, hence the name.

Tartine de Clou * 7b 80ft ◊
A parallel line to the right of "Ted" is marginally easier.

Gainsbar à la Barre *** 6c 120ft ◊
A horizontal traverse on fingery flakes and illusive footholds. Timid seconds should look elsewhere for their sport.

Schwarzenegger *** 1=7c, 1+2=8a 110ft ◊
Done as a single pitch this gives one of the most sustained routes at Freyr.

Ninja ** 7c+ 80ft ◊
The initial pitch of **Schwarzenegger** with a the addition of a technical little traverse out right to "bring on the pump".

Bayou Minou ** 8a 80ft ◊
A technical bulging wall and a thin traverse into the orifice known as "the eye of Moscow".

Full Force ** 8a 70ft ◊
The ochre streak leads to the leaning crux wall to gain "the eye of Moscow".

Morgan de Toit ** 8a 70ft ◊
A tough wall and bulge with a crux sequence that should bring back sweet memories to those who have done **Obscene Gesture**. Moving right into the cave of **Univers Zéro** is taboo at the grade. Yoyo from "the eye of Moscow".

On the first of the chipped holds, Les Prises Tailles, 6a+ (E3 5c), L'AL LEGNE
Climber: Andy Watts

Soleil du Matin ** 7b 70ft ◊

A route approached from the cliff top, ensure you are in the right place! Tough face climbing in a position of great exposure. Can your head cope with it?

71

Exiting from the initial groove on Le Rab Direct, 6a (E1 5b), L'AL LEGNE Climber: Dave Spencer

Vibrato *** 8a 130ft ◊

One of the few routes to run the full height of this section of cliff; an immensely varied and very tough pitch. The hardest three star route on the cliff, flash this and you may as well go home.

Karkass ** 1+2=8a, 2=7c+

Another route that utilises the whole face with a possible stance at half height if the whole thing proves to be a bit much.

The right edge of the stripy wall is formed by a corner running up to the right edge of the mid-height roof. This is tackled by:

Les Prises Taillées *** 6a+ (E3 5c) 140ft

A bizarre route climbing "impossible" rock on a set of the most amazing man-made holds, the product of a true craftsman. It is worth noting that after rain the jugs are usually full of water! Start on top of a pedestal reached by a short awkward scramble from the right using some "naughty" footholds.

Climb a rather harrowing flake on the right then swing left onto the first of the "chipadeedoodah's". Strenuous moves lead to the roof where a gripping blind grope should locate the finest chipped hold in the world, bar none. Cut loose and continue up the sustained wall using the occasional natural hold, past a possible stance/yoyo point to the cliff top.

The next collection of climbs on L'Al Legne are all single pitch routes situated at the far right side of the cliff. The area is easily reached from above, catches the afternoon sun and is an ideal venue to round the day off, or to grab a couple of quickies when time is tight. The left side of the wall is bounded by a excellent and long left-facing groove system:

Le Rab Direct ** 6a (E1 5b) 110ft
A fine sustained pitch with the crux right at the very top. Enter the groove awkwardly and follow it by sustained bridging and jamming until it is possible to swing onto the right arête. Continue to a shallow bay below the cliff top then step right to finish with difficulty.

Le Rab * 5 (HVS 5a) 110ft
Start as for the regular route until it exits from the groove. From here trend right up slabby rock to reach the bottom left corner of a stepped overhang. Follow this rightwards to the top.

L'Appendix * 5+ (HVS 5a) 100ft
To the right of **Le Rab Direct** is a shorter left-facing corner which gives a short slippery struggle to easier terrain. Finish as for **Le Rab**.

To the right is a smooth slab with a line of bolts up it:

Les Pantins de L'Apocalypse * 6b (E3 6a) 90ft ◊
An eliminate line that is not without interest. Gain a hole from the right then make thin fingery moves until forced rightwards into the next route. Step back left then climb direct to the belays below the cliff top.

Right again is a disjointed flake system that is climbed by;

L'Ascendante ** 4+ (VS 4c) 80ft P ◊
A good but well-glossed pitch. Follow the flake leftwards then make tricky moves up and right to reach its extension. Up this to its end then easier climbing leads past ledges to the belays.

Les Noisettes 5 (VS 5a) 60ft ◊
At the right edge of the cliff is a left-facing dièdre which is climbed to its closure. From here trend left up easier rock.

The final routes described on this cliff are those that are most easily reached from the cliff top by abseil. Double ropes will be required (make sure they will pull down), or a third party to untie your climbing rope and drop it down to you. It should be obvious that cliff top approaches open the way for countless epics. It is worth ensuring that you are in the right place and that the rope reaches your intended starting point! It will not have escaped devotees of the Verdon that these routes are ideal candidates for top-roping. Whatever you intend **BEWARE OF TEAMS BELOW.** All these routes can be approached from below if desired.

Le Zig-zag *** 5+ (HVS) 150ft P (see p56)

A spectacular main pitch on great holds starting from the final stance on **La Directissima** and weaving away up the smooth-looking face on the left.

> **1. 100ft 5+ (5b)** Climb the groove for 20ft to a cramped niche where an obvious easy traverse runs out left. Sidestep along this until a good line of polished pocket holds runs up the steep slab to a massive "blobby" peg. From the peg make an intricate finger traverse left (crux) until it is possible to swing into a short open groove which is climbed to a stance on the left.
>
> **2. 50ft 4 (4b)** Follow the obvious crack line to the cliff top.

Turbo Cool * 6a (E2 5c) 60ft

A brief but enjoyable piece of exercise in a dramatic setting. From the final stance on **Le Zig-zag** step right onto the slab and climb it trending first right then back left to finish over the capping roof.

Les Trois Saurets ** 6b+ (E3 6b) 70ft P

A short but taxing piece of climbing started most easily from the final stance on **Le Zig-zag.** Step down and reverse the traverse back to the fat peg, then climb the wall to three small holes. Desperate moves are made up and right to reach a horizontal break and a crack which leads more easily to the top. A left-hand variation from the three holes is even harder. This climb was something of a test piece for many years, it is interesting to note that it has been soloed, climbed in the dark and climbed using ice axe and crampons!

J'Ai Tout Pour Plaire ** 7a+ 120ft

Brilliant technical climbing; for the connoisseur of the mono-doigt this route has some treats in store. From the final stance on **La Directissima** climb the **Variante du Zig-zag** to the good ledge where the regular route goes straight up to the big peg. Step right and climb the steep slab to good holds then continue up smooth (and I mean smooth) rock past two small overlaps to an exit on the left: intense.

L'Enfant * 6b+ (E3 6b) 100ft

The flying arête to the right of the final pitch of **La Directissima** gives another traditional test-piece, a real boulder problem in the sky, being short, sharp and "out there". From the final stance on **L'Enfant** climb the groove in the leaning right wall of the corner (some suspect rock) or avoid this section by climbing the main corner and stepping out to the right past a optional stance onto the very edge of the known World. The arête is both technical and spectacular, and the substantial fixed gear is "sportingly" placed.

Extrême Idée *** 7a+ 120ft

A stunning pitch which is basically a long direct start to **L'Enfant**. Start from the final stance of **La Directissima**. Traverse out onto the right wall of the corner and climb this strenuously over a clutch of overhangs until it is possible to gain the bulging crest of the arête. Continue up this leftwards until it is feasible to swing round the corner to the optional stance on **L'Enfant**. Continue easily!! up this to the cliff top.

Utopia *** 7a 100ft

Another peerless pitch in an outrageous setting. Start from the exposed final stance of **L'Échec du Siècle**.

Follow the diagonal overlap into the centre of the "slab" and climb its centre to reach (with good fortune and fortitude) a thin crack. Finish more easily.

Kid Moulinette *** 7b 130ft

An eliminate that links the overhanging lower crux of **Extrême Idée** with the face climbing the upper crux of **Utopia** by its own tricky sequence. Exposed, varied and quite superb.

Lunatic Dance ** 7a+ 100ft

Starting from the final stance of **L'Échec du Siècle** is perhaps the "most exposed" of all the "very exposed" routes at Freyr.

Climb the short crux slab of L'Échec then trend right across the bulging wall until it is possible to climb straight up until close to the arête. Trend left from here up the tilted side wall over a bulge to the cliff top. Wild, wild, wild situations.

The next three routes described start from the stance on top of Le Pilastre which can be reached by an awkward diagonal abseil down the final groove of the route of the same name.

Double You * 6c 60ft

From the final stance of **Le Pilastre** traverse out left and climb the smooth wall by devious moves. The final section can be done on the left (6c) or on the right (6c+).

Propaganda *** 7c 100ft

Climb the streaked wall behind the stance to a series of bulges which are tackled direct to a semi-rest at an overlap. Finish up the final smooth wall.

La Cerise from Le Pilastre *** 7a 100ft

The top two thirds of the final superb pitch of La Cerise can be approached from here if you can't face the walk down to the foot of the cliff to do the rest of the route! Unfortunately (or otherwise) this approach misses out the hardest moves.

From the top of Le Pilastre move out right round a technical bulge to gain a wall and climb this to the rainbow shaped overlap. Undercut round to the left end of this then trend left up the wall to easier rock.

Art of Noise ** 7a+ 120ft

Start at a poor stance 20 feet down the easy groove on the right side of Le Pilastre. **Going Wild 6c (E4 6a)** is a logical way to get here from the base of the cliff, or climb down from the top of the tower.

Move right then climb straight up the bulging wall until it is possible to trend left to the right edge of the rainbow shaped overlap on the previous route. From here step right and pull through the bulges to enter a shallow groove that leads to easier climbing and the cliff top. Very well protected, take plenty of quick-draws.

To the south of the view point there are two large fins of rock that protrude towards the river from the wooded hillside. The more northerly one is the **Rocher de Louis-Phillipe** and the southerly one is the **Rocher de la Jeunesse**. Both these buttresses are quite difficult to pick out from above because of the trees, though when seen from the other side of the river they are easily recognised because of the alarming way that they both list to the right. The angle of both cliffs means that large sections can be climbed on when it is raining as some areas of the rock stay dry. Unfortunately the same can not be said for the approach paths to both cliffs which can become suicidally slippery after rain. Under these conditions a good pair of cleated soles is a sensible idea, and smooth soled trainers are not!

LE LOUIS-PHILIPPE

INTRODUCTION

A steep and interesting cliff that is south-facing and is home to a good collection of powerful lines. The quality of the rock is very agreeable and despite being close to the car park the cliff is usually quiet. The routes are described from right to left as they are approached down the gully that runs below the cliff all the way to the riverside path. Be warned, as mentioned above, it can be very slippery after rain.

GEOGRAPHY

The Louis-Philippe runs steeply down the side of the gully and flat ground for gearing up is at a premium, the best spot being in the ever-dry recess below **Voie des Trous**. The crag can be conveniently divided into three sections. First, high on the right side of the cliff is a huge double overhang **(Le Toit du Monde)**, below and to the right of this is a grassy ledge that can be reached by an easy scramble from the right. A small collection of climbs start here. Second is the large central section of the cliff containing an eye-catching set of groove lines and impressive bulges. The flat wall of the classic **Capt'aine Coeur de Miel** is further down the gully and it bounds the left side of this central section of the face. Finally, close to the bottom of the gully, are a small set of leaning walls and bulges with a small choice of routes.

APPROACHES

From the lowest point of the car park by the lookout (see map) follow a path leftwards into the woods (this is the track that goes to the camping field). After 50m a track branches down to the right, by a notice on a tree, and descends diagonally leftwards to a rocky step. This is the point where the ridge of the cliff runs into the hillside. The first section of rock lurks just around the corner but for the main section of the crag it is best to follow the path diagonally down to the next rocky outcrop (the top of **La Jeunesse**) and then tack back across the gully. Direct descents of the gully are likely to end up with monumental bum-slides ending up somewhere near the river. You have been warned (more than once).

The first climbs described are situated high on the right side of the cliff. There is only a small collection of pitches here and they are generally quite tough and rather short. However the cliff is in the sun late in the day and the grassy ledge is a good place to "grab a few rays", or to take the evening air. If you are looking for a short tough project that is easy to get at, look no further. There are bolt belays on the slabby ledge below the wall and considering the considerable drop below the ledge it is probably worth using them! The climbs are described from right to left.

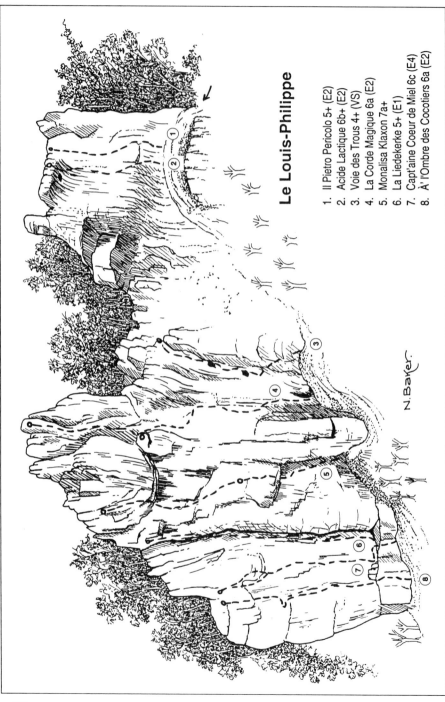

Le Louis-Philippe

1. Il Pietro Pericolo 5+ (E2)
2. Acide Lactique 6b+ (E2)
3. Voie des Trous 4+ (VS)
4. La Corde Magique 6a (E2)
5. Monalisa Klaxon 7a+
6. La Liedekerke 5+ (E1)
7. Capt'aine Coeur de Miel 6c (E4)
8. À l'Ombre des Cocotiers 6a (E2)

N. Baker

Alice au Pays des Merveilles 5 (E1 5b) 40ft ◊
The right-hand line is the least worthwhile on this section of cliff. Start just right of an open scoop and climb the bulging rib on "interesting" rock: a rather friable conglomeration of fossils loosely cemented together.

Il Pietro Pericolo ** 5+ (E2 5c) 40ft ◊
A good steep outing, harder than it looks and offering some pleasant pocket pulling. Start left of the open groove in the right side of the face and climb past a patch of yellow rock (just a touch bold) then head up the face by using a series of continually surprising holds to lower offs just over the rim.

Acide Lactique ** 6b+ (E2 6a or E3 5c depending on your penchant) 40ft ◊
Start at the third bolt line from the right. Make a couple of difficult moves over the initial bulge left then right, then follow easier rock to below the capping cornice. The holds on this are huge apart from the first one; lean out backwards, grab the jugs then go for it before you drown in tidal waves of ......

Lubna ** 6c (E4 6a) 40ft ◊
Start as for the previous climb but pull left over the initial bulge then trend left up the leaning wall by sustained steep climbing on mostly good holds. A pumpy little number that is rather sequential.

Lubna Direct * 7a+ 40ft ◊
Approach the upper part of the previous route via a short and exceptionally sharp direct start. Once over the bulge cruise the regular route. It is usual, though not essential, to pre-clip the first two bolts.

Terminus, Tout le Monde Descend * 7c 40ft ◊
A left-hand start to the previous route is always well chalked up but doesn't see many ascents, it is something to do with the ridiculous angle and the pathetic holds on offer.

Le Toit du Monde * A1 50ft
The large overhangs are one of the few routes at Freyr where you can indulge in that ancient pastime of aid climbing. If you are not sure what that is, consult any of the old text books, sort out some knotted slings and then get swinging.

Quomologma ** 8a 50ft ◊
The left to right diagonal through the huge double roofs is one of the most spectacular routes at Freyr; it's also pretty tough. A route for the dedicated and talented only.

La Mignonne * 3 (Severe) 60ft

The ramp that runs left under the roofs gives a pleasant and exposed outing. From the grass ledge climb leftwards along the obvious line to round the arête then descend to the col. The route can then be reversed at the same grade and double the length.

The next collection of climbs is located on the right side of the central section of the cliff. They start from a rounded, flat-floored bay, with a protruding pillar with a prominent flat roof on its left side.

Tarzouille 5+ (E1 5c) 50ft ◊

The right side of the bay has a short steep wall containing some large closely spaced bolts. Climb into the initial scoop (crux) then pull out of this leftwards on good holds. Continue up steep but easier rock slightly rightwards to the lower off.

Voie des Trous * 4+ (VS 5a) P ◊

Climb the left trending slabby ramp in the back of the bay to enter the prominent wide groove system that slants back to the right. After examining both holes (the second of which offers an escape route through the cliff if the route proves too much) climb the crux bulge by technical bridging then continue more easily to a lower off in the right rib of the groove. It is also possible to continue all the way to the cliff top if you have got the scent of the summit in your nostrils.

In the back left side of the bay is an open groove that leads to a steep discontinuous crack line running up the cliff and fading out into steeper rock. This is the start of **La Corde Magique**. Just to the right of this is the unlikely looking line of:

Professeur Bras de Beurre ** 6a (E2 5c) 70ft ◊

Climb the easy slab directly into the bay of the previous route then swing out left onto the steep pillar at the level of a cemented peg. Steep blind moves lead up this (easy if you locate the holds, desperate if not) to a semi rest. Move left and climb a short, awkward and slippery crack to a good protruding stance on the Nombril ("the navel", I suppose there is a passing resemblance) on the left. Lower off.

Y'a Pas d'Heures Pour les Braves * 7a 80ft ◊

The obvious leaning direct finish to the previous climb above its resting place is short, steep and sharp.

La Corde Magique ** 6a (E2) 130ft

1. 70ft 6a (5c) P ◊ Climb the shallow groove on the left side of the bay, then step right into the thin crack. (Yes the first bolt is a long way off the ground isn't it!) Continue up this then step left and climb a short awkward and slippery jamming crack in a corner to a good stance on the Nombril.

2. 60ft 5+ (5b) ◊ The traditional finish is the desperate, short-lived and ultimately unsatisfying groove on the left of the stance **6b+ (6b)**. **Le Turban** is a direct finish that is more in keeping with the rest of the climb. Step right and climb the steep groove on good holds to gain a left-trending ramp. Above the start of this is an overhanging rib that is climbed on massive but rather spaced holds (a real gorilla thriller) to the cliff top. Either abseil off or walk round.

To the left is a protruding pillar with a prominent small flat roof. A couple of short pleasant pitches reaches the ledge on top of the pillar by passing either side of the roof. From here it is usual to lower off though it is possible to continue up **Le Fakir** (see below).

Variante de Départ Droite * 30ft 5+ (E1 5b) ◊
Climb leftwards towards the right edge of the roof then continue up the short wall on good small holds to the ledge.

Variante de Départ Gauche 30ft 6a (E2 5c) ◊
The crack splitting the roof just to the left gives a short awkward struggle.

To the left are twin grooves that run out into much steeper rock high above. The right-hand groove is the usual start to the ancient (1939) classic of

Le Fakir ** 5+ (E2) 140ft P
1. 80ft 5+ (5c) ◊ Follow the groove steeply until it is possible to step right onto the rib for a breather. Continue up into the hanging niche above with difficulty and exit right on to the Nombril. The left-hand groove can also be climbed followed by a short traverse to the right to join the regular route. Judging by the name there must be somewhere on this pitch to do "an Egyptian", I obviously missed it.
2. 60ft 5 (5a) Step right and climb the short steep wall on good holds to gain access to the left trending ramp line which is followed in fine position to the cliff top. Either abseil off or walk round.

To the left of the left-hand start to **Le Fakir** is a large flat roof with a prominent bolt just above its lip. This provides the first pitch of the spectacular

Monalisa Klaxon *** 7a+ 120ft ◊
1. 50ft 6b (6a) ◊ Climb to the roof and cross it leftwards before climbing up to a palatial stance. A great place to watch the fun and games from.
2. 90ft 7a+ ◊ Follow the straightforward groove above the stance until the rock begins to bulge. Trend left under the largest overhang then climb directly up the leaning rib on small holds until it is possible to head up and rightwards to enter a groove that leads with a little less exertion to the lowering point. A magnificent pitch and a monumental pumper.

The long groove line to the left starts from a flat ledge and is the classic **La Liedekerke**. Starting just to the right of the groove is
Aéroplane Blindé ** 7a 100ft ◊
Follow the line of bolts up the rib and over a clutch of bulges until it is possible to bridge (or crawl!) into the prominent groove which leads to a lowering point.

La Liedekerke * 5+ (E1 5b) 90ft** ◊
The long groove gives a distinguished pitch. Climb awkwardly onto a flat ledge with bolt belay. The groove is entered steeply using a great selection of massive holds and then gives a good honest pitch of jamming and bridging to reach eventually lowering bolts in the right wall. More classical than ancient Greece.

To the left is a flat pocketed wall that contains three short but excellent pitches. The lower section of the wall is crossed by a ledge which can be reached by a short awkward scramble from the right (as for **La Liedekerke**) or from directly below up a black slab as a way of extending the routes.

Capt'aine Coeur de Miel *
6c (E4 6a) 70ft** ◊
One of Freyr's classic 6cs. From the groove of **La Liedekerke** step left and climb the steep pockety wall to reach a thin overlap. Cross this leftwards with difficulty then make an uphill and blind swing into the groove on the left to reach an easier finish. The final section can also be climbed direct at **6c+ (E5 6a)** if you thought the lower section of the route a soft touch.

Entering the classic groove line of La Liedekerke, 5+ (E1 5b) LE LOUIS-PHILIPPE. Climber: Chris Craggs

À L'Ombre des Cocotiers ** 6a (E2 5c) 70ft ◊

Great climbing up a line of giant holes. Climb the initial dark slab past a peg runner to the ledge cutting across the lower section of the wall. From here follow the line of deep pockets rising leftwards up the wall until the rock steepens up. Make a difficult move up and left to a ledge then more difficult moves (crux) back to the right around the rib and into the easier finishing groove.

La Fuite au Cul *** 6a (E2 5b) 70ft ◊

Climb the initial dark slab past a peg runner to the ledge then step left and climb the steep wall on generous holds as directly as possible to a position below a bulge. A blind reach round this leads to good holds, then just when you thought it was in the bag, what a dirty trick: the crux. Enter the scoop above the bulge using a very retiring mono-doigt, then finish easily.

The final section of Louis-Philippe is to be found very close to the bottom of the gully where there is a short leaning buttress with a few worthwhile routes on it. These can be reached by descending the gully below the main cliff or by walking round from the foot of La Jeunesse. The routes are described from right to left for consistency.

La Ragazza de Finale 6b (E3 6a) 30ft ◊

At the right side of the wall is a low cave and to the left of this is a narrow leaning wall with four closely-spaced bolts in it. The final moves to the lower off prove to be the crux.

Topolina ** 6a (E1 5c) 40ft ◊

A steep little pitch with a lot of good holds.

To the left is a long right slanting groove line. Start to the right of the base of this below an undercut rib. Make a fingery pull (crux) then climb up to a rest in the groove. Cross this and climb up the leaning wall on its left and over an imposing bulge above to the belays. Less direct variations are inferior.

La Honte de la Jungle *** 6b+ (E4 6a) 80ft ◊

A fine varied route with a spectacular climax.

Move left from on top of the block to the left of **Topolina** and swing across the bottom of the steep groove to gain a ramp (big beckoning bolt) that spirals up the rib to the left. From the end of this climb easier rock to the foot of a steep white wall and continue up this to a bulge. Pull over the bulge then trend right up the leaning wall, on mostly good holds, in an amazing position. The direct finish from the bulge sprouts a few ancient pegs and awaits a person of vision who owns a big battery-powered drill.

Down the slope to the left, before the cliff fizzles out is a short wall with a steep corner on its right side and a huge hanging flake in its centre. The corner is

83

L'Horreur dans le Musée * 6a+ (E2 5c) 30ft ◊

A short lived piece of exercise that is not without interest. The groove is bridged steeply with the crux moves reaching or passing the first bolt, all depending on how brave you feel.

Popov * 6c (E3 6c) 30ft ◊

The direct route over the bulge in the centre of the wall is a piece of technical wizardry: a real one move wonder, but what a move.

At the left edge of the wall is a left-slanting ramp, the start of

Des Pommes et des Pas Mûres ** 5 (HVS) 90ft ◊

A good little route, worth seeking out.

1. 40ft 5 (5a) ◊ Climb leftwards up the slabby ramp, make a steep pull then trend back right to climb over the huge dubious-looking flake (it looks dubious enough when you are perched on its tip, clipped into the bolt that is attached to the flake). Climb over a bulge to a good stance.

2. 50ft 4 (4c) ◊ Move steeply up the right side of the arête on good holds until it is possible to pull round to the left and follow the rather floral slab to belay in a notch just below the top of the tower. Either scramble over the crest to easy ground or make a hairy 80ft abseil from the belays.

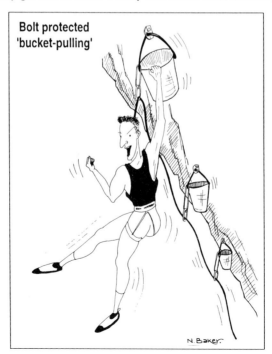

Bolt protected 'bucket-pulling'

N. Baker

LA JEUNESSE

INTRODUCTION

A cliff that initially appears rather small and of limited interest. On close acquaintance it proves to be an extensive, complex and very steep south-facing piece of rock with an excellent selection of climbs. Most grades are well catered for and there are some especially worthwhile middle grade routes that weave their way up steep rock in a way guaranteed to provide exciting classic climbing. The steepness of the central section of the wall means that large parts of the cliff stay dry during rain. Protection is plentiful and always solid.

GEOGRAPHY

The cliff presents a flat and, on first acquaintance, a rather featureless face, rising above the steep slope. On the far right is a steep groove running into vegetated rock and left of this are two steep open grooves, both yellowish in colour. The left-hand one runs up to a cave opening high on the cliff; **La Rue de la Paix**. Left of this is a steeper wall with an **A**-shaped recess cutting through its lower section and offering an approach to the base of two steep ramps that form a **V**. The left one is taken by **La Nouvelle Jeunesse** and the right one by **La Mimi**. The very leaning wall directly above the lowest point of the **V** has the conspicuous hanging flake of **Welcome to the Machine** in its centre. Left again the lower section of the wall overhangs and has a collection of "ever-dry" routes with **Melampyre** being the pick of the bunch. The left side of the cliff is the highest and the steep slippery ramp of **La Grand-Mère** leads to steeper stuff above, most notably the prominent ragged crack-line of **La Madone**.

APPROACHES

The crag is reached by parking as for the View Point and the Louis-Philippe (see map) and following the path that leaves the bottom left corner of the parking area and runs out to reach the camping field. Fifty metres along here a path branches down to the right (sign on tree) and descends diagonally leftwards through the woods to reach a rocky shoulder; this is the point where the Rocher de la Louis-Philippe runs into the hillside. Continue more steeply in the same direction to cross over another rocky section; the point where the Jeunesse runs into the hillside and descend the gully just beyond this.

> **WARNING** (for the 4th time): after rain this path is very slippery, either wear shoes with good soles or be prepared for a bit of skiing practice.

The routes are described from RIGHT TO LEFT as you descend the slope as this is the usual direction of approach.

La Jeunesse

1. La Culbutte 4+ (VS)
2. Triste Tropiques 6a+ (E2)
3. Negresses Vertes 5+ (E1)
4. La Rue de la Paix 5+ (E1)
5. La Mimi 5+ (E1)

6. La Nouvelle Jeunesse 4 (VS)
7. Welcome to the Machine 6c (E4)
8. Melampyre 6a+ (E2)
9. La Grand-Mère, Traversée Sans Nom
   & Serge 3+ (HVS)

10. La Madone 6b (E3)
11. La Tsoin-Tsoin 6a (E2)

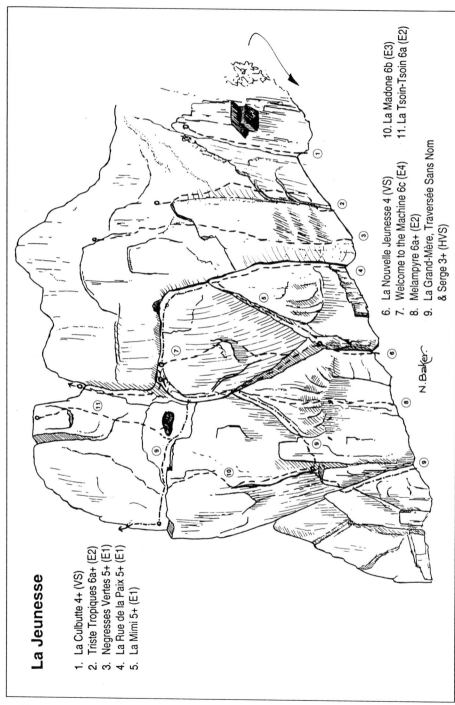

N. Baker.

The right-hand side of the cliff is bounded by a steep corner chimney springing from a cave recess. The small protruding buttress on the right of this has a pleasant pitch.

Chauves Souris ** 4 (VS 4b) 60ft ◊

Start on the right and climb leftwards over ledges to reach an open groove which leads to more ledges. Above is steeper rock, climb this first left then back right (don't worry, the big holds keep appearing) until the angle drops back and the belays can be reached. A right-hand variation of this upper section is inferior as it is rather close to the floral bank on the right.

The steep chimney groove rising from the cave is

La Culbutte * 4+ (VS 4c) 60ft ◊

A route that would doubtless be a classic in deepest Dovedale, here it is simply an "also ran". The initial section is fearsomely steep; thankfully the holds are generous. Once the easier groove is entered pleasant herbaceous bridging leads to a lower off on the right.

To the left of the chimney groove is a steep wall with two steep yellow grooves cutting up it. Immediately left of the chimney is a steep wall climbed by;

Raymond Bicochon * 4 (HVS 5a) 60ft ◊

Swing left across steep juggy rock and climb onto ledges (Grade 4???) before trending up left then back right to gain a grassy ledge awkwardly. Continue up the short wall to ledges and the lower off.

Triste Tropiques ** 6a+ (E2 6a) 80ft ◊

A varied pitch with a mono-doigt manoeuvre as its crux.

Start up the polished yellow groove 20ft left of the corner but straight away swing right and make steep thin moves up and right (crux) to reach easier rock. From here trend back to the left and climb the rib overlooking the initial groove by steep and technical climbing to reach a lower off in a shallow bay.

La Rue Lépic * 5 (HVS 5a) 70ft P ◊

Climb the steep slippery rock to gain entry to the groove (peg) and follow it to a ledge below steep rock. Step left and climb a steep flake/ramp crack to its apex then head up the steep pocketed wall for 20ft to a lower off.

It is also possible to traverse left from the tip of the flake for 80ft by following a line of flakes across the very steep and exposed wall and then continue along grassy ledges to arrive at the Col des Épinards on the crest of the wall, **5+ (E1 5b)**.

The left side of the leaning wall to the left of the first yellow groove is in the form of a broad blunt arête with two bolt lines up it. These are followed by two long and sustained pitches up the gently tilted wall:

Gêne des Alpages *** 5 (HVS 5a) 140ft ◊

A massive and excellent pitch that goes all the way to the crest of the wall. 15 quick-draws should suffice. If you run out there is a stance and belay on the left at 100ft.

Climb the initial steep wall slightly to the right then blast straight up to the top of the initial ramp on **La Rue Lepic**. From here climb the steep wall on great holds to enter the prominent cave. Pull straight out of this then follow easier rock (possible stance on the left) to a tricky overhang and then the top of the wall. Talk about rope drag. Either abseil from bolts here or traverse the crest of the ridge rightwards back to the hillside.

Negresses Vertes ** 5+ (E1 5b) 100ft

The left-hand bolt line offers excellent climbing, though perhaps not quite as good as its immediate neighbour. Climb the initial steep arête then continue straight up an interesting wall to the base of the flake/ramp on **La Rue Lepic**. Climb the steep wall above on good holds to gain a lowering point at twin bolts. It is also possible to belay here then traverse right for 10ft and follow the upper section of **Gêne des Alpages** to the cliff top. Either abseil from bolts here or traverse the crest of the ridge rightwards back to the hillside.

La Rue de la Paix ** 5+ (E1 5b) 110ft P ◊

To the left is a more prominent rounded yellow groove, trending left and with an obvious smooth section at 60ft. This gives a good pitch though the crux often sports a wet streak after rain. The groove is followed with sustained interest and one quite pushy section where it starts to bulge before it is possible to move left to reach the small cave of La Grotte Mimi. When rested traverse the obvious break leftwards (exposed 5a) to a belay on the good ledge known as the Ristorente. From here the cliff top can be reached by the final pitch of **La Mimi 40ft 4 (4c)** see below. Alternatively abseil from here, 100ft to the ground.

Down the slope from the rounded groove taken by **La Rue de la Paix** is an obvious steep break in the form of an inverted niche leading through bulges to easier angled rock below an impressively leaning diamond shaped wall. The steep wall between this niche and **La Rue de la Paix** contains two short but worthwhile pitches.

La Pétanque Sous Les Tropiques ** 6a (E2 5c) ◊

20ft left of the groove climb the fingery leaning wall past bolts and cemented pegs to gain easier rock. Up this to a lower off on the ramp of **La Mimi**. It is also possible to belay here and continue via **Nougat Rock 6a (E3 5c)** see below.

Cécile Sproutchs Raide * 5+ (E1 5b) 60ft ◊

Start under the left side of the leaning wall and climb straight up before swinging awkwardly left (OK it might only be **HVS 5a**) then trend right up the arête to a lower off on the ramp above.

The inverted weakness directly below the hanging diamond-shaped wall is known as **Jongen's Start** after its first ascensionist. It provides access to the lowest point of the two ramps that form a V shape, each taken by ancient classics and also to three more modern offerings on the steep wall that hangs above these ramps.

La Mimi ** 5+ (E1) 190ft P

The right-hand ramp is taken by this first-rate route of 1949 vintage that zigzags its way up the centre of the cliff.

1. 40ft 4 (4c) ◊ Climb the steep, slippery and awkward overhanging crack to gain access to the delights above. A belay is available directly below the steep wall, or press on.

2. 110ft 5+ (5b) ◊ Climb the fine ramp rightwards to its apex then climb the steep groove on the right, the crux section of **La Rue de la Paix**, until it is feasible to pull out left to a possible constricted stance at La Grotte Mimi ◊. From here follow the obvious exposed traverse out to the left to gain the comfortable ledge of La Ristorente.

3. 40ft 4 (4c) Climb the short steep wall on the left to reach an easy groove that leads to La Col des Epinards. Escape along the crest of the ridge (200ft) or descend by a 150ft abseil.

La Nouvelle Jeunesse *** 4 (VS) 160ft P

An even more venerable way up the cliff (1938), offering amicably-graded climbing that pierces the very heart of the cliff.

1. 40ft 4 (4c) Climb the steep slippery and awkward overhanging crack (easier on the right) to gain access to the delights above. This is hard work but it is worth persevering. A belay is available right under the overhanging wall.

2. 80ft 3+ (4b) Follow the left slanting ramp to its top and then step left to climb a steep exposed rib into a groove. Pull over an awkward bulge a comfortable stance on the right with multifarious belays. This is the Ristorente though you will probably find that tea is not being served!

3. 40ft 4 (4c) Climb the short steep wall on the left (spaced biffos) to reach an easy groove that leads to Le Col des Épinards. Escape over the crest of the ridge (200ft) or descend by a 150ft abseil.

The next three climbs involve themselves with the leaning diamond-shaped wall that hangs above the starting groove of the previous two routes. They all start up the first pitch of **La Mimi** to an optional but recommended belay at the base of the wall.

Nougat Rock * 6a (E3 5c) 120ft ◊

A climb that makes up in positions what it lacks in line. Most certainly not a route for timid seconds. Follow the second pitch of **La Mimi** to the top of the ramp where an obvious break can be seen running out across the tilted wall to the left. Follow this by swinging along on superb holds for 40ft until it is possible to join and follow **Tokapi** to the Ristorente. Abseil or lower off, or continue to the cliff top.

Welcome To The Machine ** 6c (E4 6a) 100ft ◊

A great pitch set well the wrong side of vertical, a must for Pink Floyd fans and those who like "hanging loose". In the centre of the leaning wall there is a prominent short flake crack going nowhere. Gain this from the left then either loop slightly right or make a massive reach straight up. Continue on superb holds to the lower off at the right edge of the Ristorente. Shorties might feel the route deserves UK 6b.

Tokapi ** 6a (E2 5b) 100ft ◊

Climb the left slanting ramp of **La Nouvelle Jeunesse** (or the harder slab just a little further left) until 10ft from its top. Swing right onto the steep wall (rather bold-feeling) then plough on straight up it on a continually surprising set of holds to various lower offs at the Ristorente.

To the left and down the slope from the inverted V groove of **Jongen's Start** is a steep wall with a line of bulges across it at two thirds height. There are five rather crowded pitches on here that give good ever-dry sport at reasonable grades. Three of the climbs end up at the top of the ramp above this lower wall and the other two press on up the short continuation wall above to reach the amazing Grotte de la Jeunesse. The right edge of this section is actually the left wall of the starting groove of **La Mimi** etc, and the leaning centre of this is tackled by:

Tunderflash ** 6a (E2 5c) 80ft ◊

Climb the tilted wall using good but well spaced holds to a grasping move onto a ledge, then continue up the bulging arête above with one more interesting (crux!) move to reach left-trending easy rock. Lower off from the top of the ramp or (more in line) from the bolt to the right of the cave entrance.

The arête immediately left is **Poupée Rose * 6a+ (E2 6a) 80ft ◊** which has a couple of tough moves before it joins and finishes up **Tunderflash**.

Melampyre *** 6a+ (E2 5c) 90ft ◊

This route tackles the centre of this section of the wall by a steep ragged crack line and then pulls through the middle of the bulges (crux) to get onto the upper part of the wall. Up this to lower from bolts on the rim of the ramp (70ft) or continue to the Grotte de la Jeunesse as for the previous route and lower from here.

Powerful climbing on the hanging flake of Welcome to the Machine, 6c (E4 6a), LA JEUNESSE

À L'Ombre de la Pluie ** 6a (E1 5b) 100ft ◊

Left again climb the second bolt ladder from the left edge of this section of wall (ring bolt belay at the bottom of the wall). Trend left then back right to pull through a bulge and onto the ramp that rises rightwards across this section of cliff. Move right up this then climb the short wall just left of the top of the ramp to the lowering point by the Grotte de la Jeunesse. The short steep upper wall can be avoided on the right or by lowering from bolts on the ramp with a slight reduction in grade.

Manon ** 6a (E2 5c) 90ft ◊

A varied pitch with a couple of manifestly butch moves on the upper wall. Take the bolt line just right of the slabby groove that bounds this section of wall on the left and climb to and through the left edge of the bulges to gain access to the ramp and a possible stance, (E1 5b) thus far. Move right and attack the steep wall making a difficult span out left to reach a large flake before climbing straight up the wall to attain the Grotte de la Jeunesse.

To the left is a glossy slabby chimney-ramp that rises leftwards up the cliff. This is the initial pitch of one of the great traditional classics of the area and it also provides access to a couple of distinguished climbs that are located on the wall above.

La Grand-Mère, La Traversée Sans Nom & La Traversée Serge * 3+ (HVS) 460ft**. A great route that follows a cheeky line up the highest part of the

On the ramp of La Traversée Sans Nom, 3+ (HVS 5b), LA JEUNESSE.
Climber: Sherri Davy

cliff, and gives you the chance to get three ticks in one go! It has good stances and protection but is very exposed in places. A couple of points of aid, as and when required, would reduce the overall grade considerably. Don't blame me for the Belgian grades of some of the pitches!

1. 40ft   2 (Severe)   La Grand-Mère P ◊ Climb the awkward chimney-ramp past a bulge until it is possible to traverse right over a series of spikes to a small stance with superb belays below the leaning wall.

2. 80ft   3+ (5b)   La Traversée Sans Nom P ◊ Step right into the corner then move steeply across to the bulging and polished wall on the right (crux) to reach the beckoning ramp line and follow it into the hub of the cliff.

At the top of the ramp climb over a bulge and then step left onto a shelving ledge and make a short awkward traverse out left to reach one of the world's more amazing stances, La Grotte de la Jeunesse. The faint of heart will find an escape route from here through the cliff by dint of a bit of "ratting".

It is also possible to move right to a belay on a wire cable and bolts from where it is possible to reach the cliff top via the top pitch of **La Nouvelle Jeunesse** 4 (4c) (see above) but that would miss out two of the highlights of the route.

3. 50ft   3 (4b)   La Traversée Serge Climb back out of the cave and traverse left along the obvious and very exposed line until it is possible to belay just around the corner away from that nasty drop. There isn't much protection on this pitch, but then again it isn't very hard, just don't fall off!

4. 90ft   3 (5a) Step back right and climb the short steep wall, pegs, to gain the crest of the ridge. Belay on top of the tower.

5 etc. 200ft V.Diff Follow the crest of the ridge carefully down into the Col des Epinards (possible stance) and continue in fine position across the spine of the cliff all the way back to the hillside and safety.

Scaramouch *** 6a+ (E3 6a) 180ft

1. 40ft   2 (Severe) Climb La Grand-Mère to a stance below the leaning wall.

2. 140ft 6a+ (5c) Climb the steep crack above the stance slightly leftwards for 20ft as for **La Madone** crux (see below) to the good resting place. From here a line of flakes trending rightwards up the wall can be followed on superb holds to a breather mid-way along the ledge system of **La Traversée Serge**. When suitably refreshed continue up the head wall to a stance on the ridge. The pitch contains 15 bolt runners and is quite superb.

La Madone *** 6b (E3 6a) 110ft ◊

A great classic up the soaring crack line in the wall above the polished ramp.

1. 40ft   2 (Severe) Climb **La Grand-Mère** to a well-appointed stance below the leaning wall.

2. 70ft   6b (6a) Climb leftwards up the crack in the wall behind the stance (try stepping in from the right), it feels steeper than it looks, and it looks pretty steep. A difficult undercut move gains an excellent rest on some large flakes. From here continue up the crack until forced to make a difficult swing right (crux) to massive holds. A short sprint and then the climbing eases and a bit of a romp is possible to reach the stance at the left end of **La Traversée Serge**. Lower off and get an insight as to why the route was hard work or do **La Fra Diavolo** (see below) which climbs the wall above.

The next three climbs are to be found on the fine wall set high on the cliff above **La Traversée Serge**. The easiest access to them is either by doing one or other of the routes on the lower wall, or coming through the 'back door' of La Grotte de la Jeunesse. Doubtless they could be approached from above if you fancied a real epic. They are described right to left in keeping with the rest of the cliff:

La Tsoin-Tsoin ** 6a (E2 5c) 80ft ◊

A good pitch with a unique start. From a belay in La Grotte de la Jeunesse pull onto the wall above (instant exposure) to cross a left-ward trending ramp. Continue straight up to pull over the right edge of a small overhang and continue to the ridge. How you escape from here is up to you.

La Belle Récompense * 5- (HVS 5a) 90ft

An enjoyable pitch in a gripping setting. Carry a few wires. Start from a belay at the left end of the ledge system of **La Traversée Serge**. Climb diagonally rightwards across the centre of the wall on superb holds and in a dramatic situation until it is possible to step round into a groove and climb this to the cliff top. The final groove can also be approached from above the short steep wall on **La Nouvelle Jeunesse**, to which it provides an alternative finish at **4+(VS 4c)**.

La Fra Diavolo ** 5+ (E1 5b) 80ft ◊

Start from the same stance as the previous route at the left end of the ledge system of **La Traversée Serge**.

Climb diagonally rightwards across the fine wall to gain its centre then climb direct to the cliff top.

To the left of the polished ramp of **La Grande-Mère** is the last section of rock of any interest on this face. It takes the form of a steep open groove rising from a flat-floored recess, something of a rarity in these parts. In the back of the groove is a steep jamming crack marked by three bolts. There are several short pleasant routes here. The right arête of the recess is climbed by one of the better ones:

La Belle-Mère * 5+ (E1 5c) 40ft ◊

The rib is climbed past four peg runners with a fingery crux getting past the bendy one.

La Voronov Bip Bip * 5+ (E1 5b) 100ft ◊

A long pitch with some good bits, some bad bits and some gripping bits. Climb the jamming crack in the back of the bay (a good bit) to ledges. Continue up the sandy wall (a bad bit) until a steep pull gains easier angled rock. Up this rightwards to a flake below steep rock which is best climbed quickly (you guessed it, a gripping bit) to the belays at the end of **La Traversée Serge**.

La Fra Diavolo ** 5+ (E1 5b) 80ft (see above) is one of several obvious ways on from here, or abseil off.

L'Ancienne Jeunesse *** 3 (VS) 430ft

The original route of the cliff (1931) traverses the whole crest of the crag offering a superb trip with excellent positions and only one short hard section, alpine climbing without the danger. Start just left of the very base of the cliff, just above the riverside path where an open chimney is to be found leading up to large ledges.

1. 50ft   3 (V.Diff)   Climb the chimney to a stance by a tree, other starts are possible.

2. 70ft   (Mod)   Follow the easy arête to the Col Gradine then slant left up the north face of the cliff (left side looking up) to a clump of trees at the foot of an ominous steepening that blocks the ridge, Le Grand Gendarme.

3. 90ft   3 (5a)   Climb the right side of the arête steeply for 10ft (short, sharp and eminently friggable) then pull left to regain the arête and follow it to a stance on the summit of the cliff. Who has got the flag and the Kendal Mint Cake?

4. 50ft   (Diff)   Descend the narrow ridge with care, clipping any bolt belays as runners, to a stance on Le Col des Épinards.

5. 70ft   (V.Diff)   Climb the short steep crest of the ridge to a stance on top of the final tower.

6. 100ft Descend the easy ridge back to the hillside, and the end of a great trip. If you left your rucksacks down by the river a volunteer is required!

The evolution of the Belgian bolt

ROCHERS DE NEVIAU - DAVE

INTRODUCTION

A short distance to the south of the large town of Namur there is a series of west-facing buttresses that have several features making them worth a visit; the crag is ten yards from the road, large sections of the rock never get wet, and all the routes are well bolted. The rock is a rather odd-looking black limestone, well riddled with pockets and with a rather smooth texture. The cliff is spattered with overhangs of all sizes from inconvenient bulges to massive roofs and although some of the rock looks rather blocky, in the main it is well cemented together. Dave has been popular with local climbers since the mid 1930s and some of the routes are now quite well glossed, though as much of the climbing is on good pockets this slickness does not detract too much from the pleasure of the ascent.

The setting of the cliff is rather urban. With the road being so close and the railway just a little further away it can be noisy at times. Dave lacks the grandeur of Freyr but its accessibility, broad range of routes and sunny aspect make it well worth a visit or two. People often make their first acquaintance with Dave on miserable wet days in search of dry rock. Under these conditions any cliff can be rather depressing. On the other hand a sunny evening or two spent here should give you a different feeling for the cliff.

The latest topo guide to the crag lists well over 150 routes of all grades from 2 to 7c so there is something here for most people and there is a whole heap of routes for those operating from VS to E1. Many of the names of the routes are painted on the rock.

GEOGRAPHY

At the left side of the cliff is a slabby tower separated from the main massif by a wide tree-filled gully containing an ancient concrete pill-box, this is **Les Autrichiens**, and it is home to a selection of lower grade routes as well as a few tougher ones. At the right toe of this buttress is the small tower of the **Bloc du Parachute**, a small piece of rock with a small number of harder routes. The main section of the cliff lies directly across the road from the car parking and this has a prominent pointed and tree-capped tower on its left side: the **Secteur Bons Enfants**. To the right of this is a slab leading to a clutter of roofs and grooves, the **Secteur Fontaine - Directe**, with a large left-facing wall bounding its right side. Right again is the **Secteur Central** where the upper half of the cliff is a "Hyll Drem"-like mass of overhangs some of them being pretty huge. Not unexpectedly the lower part of this rarely gets wet. There are lowering points below the roofs

---

The exposed Traversée Serge, 3 (VS 4b), LA JEUNESSE. Climber: Chris Craggs

on many of the routes so that some sport can usually be salvaged here on wet days.

Further to the right the cliff begins to lose height and interest with the slabby and rather vegetated **Massif du Bivouac** being the last section of any real worth.

APPROACHES
6km to the south of Namur and 20km north of Dinant on the east bank on the Meuse and overlooking the N92 are a series of steep buttress that tower above the trees. There is extensive parking on the opposite side of the busy road; the traffic really flies up and down here, cross with care!

The buttresses are described from left to right as are the routes on each buttress starting with the large tower at the left side of the cliff:

LES AUTRICHIENS
The pyramidal tower that forms the left extremity of the cliff has a pleasing selection of climbs, many of them well suited to novices. There are bolt runners in all the routes here, though they are sometimes well spaced. Carry a selection of large Rocks and a couple of Friends if you think you might need them. All stances are well equipped with belays and lowering rings so if you find you have bitten off more than you can chew, escape is no problem.

The simplest descent for any routes that reach the top of the tower is to follow the rocky ridge back to the hillside and then descend the easy gully to the right of the buttress.

The north side of the tower at the very left fringe of the cliff has a few routes worth seeking out.

L'Aspirant * 2 (Diff) 150ft
A prominent left-trending slab is the starting point for the easiest route on the whole cliff. It can be used by the most timid of "rabbits" and if they find this a gripper then perhaps rock climbing is not the game for them.

1. 50ft Climb the ramp to a stance where it drops back to easy ground and spacious ledges.

2. 50ft Traverse left a short distance then climb a straightforward ridge to a smaller stance on top of a pillar.

3. 50ft Traverse up and right following the obvious line to reach the crest of the buttress. Finish up this in a fine position.

The steep right wall of the initial ramp of the previous route has three closely spaced bolt lines that give quick ticks though they are best used as approaches to the two routes that battle through the frowning bulges above. Each route climbs

---

Above the initial bulges of Gier 6b (E3 6a) STEENBOKMASSIEF, MOZET. Climber: Colin Binks

past one ledge to belay on a higher one:

La Chinoise 4+ (VS 4c) 50ft ◊
The left-hand line.

Le Chicot 4+ (VS 4c) 50ft ◊
The central line.

Le Chichi 4+ (VS 4c) 50ft ◊
The right-hand line.

Above the ledge that these last three pitches finish on is a bulging wall that has two worthwhile pitches weaving their way up unlikely terrain. They are both worth the journey up to get at them.

Les Taches Jaunes ** 5+ (E1 5b) 80ft ◊
Take the left side of the wall (and right of the prominent crack) by sustained and fingery climbing on rock that is quite steep enough to "bring on the pump". The small overhang part way up the pitch adds a little extra interest. While lowering off you can have a sneak preview of the rather harder line to the right, unless you close your eyes on the way down!

Les Taches Noires * 6a (E2 5c) 80ft ◊
The right-hand line is another bit of beef cake, great climbing on good holds but oh so steep.

The river face of **Les Autrichiens** is basically a broad slab on the right with a series of corners on the left. One of the corners contains a deep wide crack (or a narrow chimney) with "miserable" painted on its right wall. This is the start of

Le Bok * 3+ (Severe) 140ft
1. 60ft   Climb the left side of the chimney-crack to pass the narrowing then follow easier ledges back up right to a good stance on bushy ledges.
2. 50ft   Step right then climb the slabby front of the square projecting rib above by weaving through the bulges to reach an exposed stance on a shoulder.
3. 30ft   Finish up the finely-positioned ridge to reach the top of the tower with its in-situ trees.

To the right is a straight crack starting behind a solitary block on the ground.

Bilboquet * 5- (VS 4c) 60ft ◊
Follow the crack over a small bulge, into a hanging corner and over a larger bulge. Above this good holds lead to ledges and a lower off. Alternatively a finish is possible up the top pitch of **Le Bok** to extend the pleasure (see above).

30ft to the right of the block on the ground is a prominent steep corner blocked by an imposing barrier of overhangs at 30ft. These features are scaled by the short but worthwhile route of

Le Grand Surplomb * 5- (HVS 5a) 40ft P ◊
Climb the polished corner and then bridge awkwardly through the bulges to reach a lower off where the angle falls back. It is possible to continue but the terrain above is somewhat overgrown.

Around to the right is the large broken slab that forms the right side of the cliff. This has three main routes on it and a number of variations.

La Joss-Land * 3 (V.Diff) 80ft ◊
The line that starts at the left toe of the slab and climbs up its left side is pleasant enough. At the ledges level with a prominent tree on the left there are various lower offs.

Les Autrichiens ** 3+ (Severe) 160ft
The original route of the face and still worth doing. Start at the centre of the slab behind the signpost.
1. 90ft   3   ◊   Climb the slab to a small bulge that bars access to a left-facing groove. Cross this (easier on the left) and continue to the ledges at the top of the slab. Move left to a stance behind bushes and below a steep groove.
2. 70ft   3+   Up the groove and continue in the same line with less difficulty to the cliff top.
2a.70ft   3+   The slab above the centre of the ledges at the top of the first pitch (belay) offers a possible variation second pitch at much the same grade and quality.

The right side of the lower slab has a series of white bulges at half height. These are tackled by

Lamoretti * 4 (H.Severe 4a) 70ft ◊
Climb straight up the easy slab then follow an awkward crack through the centre of the white band to reach steeper rock which has better holds. Lower off or select one of the routes that runs to the cliff top.

The right arête of **LES AUTRICHIENS** is the classic little expedition of

Le Cheval Rouge ** 3 (Severe) 140ft
1. 70ft   Climb the right edge of the buttress (just left of a deep chimney) then when it begins to steepen up move around right into the chimney. This is quite steep but is "well endowed" so continue with pleasure to a good stance.
2. 80ft   Follow easy ledges up to the base of the upper arête and climb this until things begin to get a little too steep for comfort. Once again the answer

Les Autrichiens - Dave

1. Le Bok 3+ (Severe)
2. Le Grand Surplomb 5- (HVS)
3. Les Autrichiens 3+ (Severe)
4. Le Cheval Rouge 3 (Severe)
5. Le Parachute 6a+ (E2)

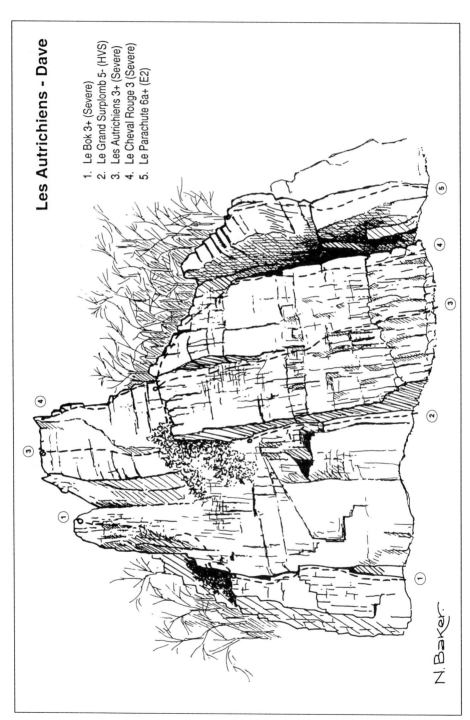

N. Baker.

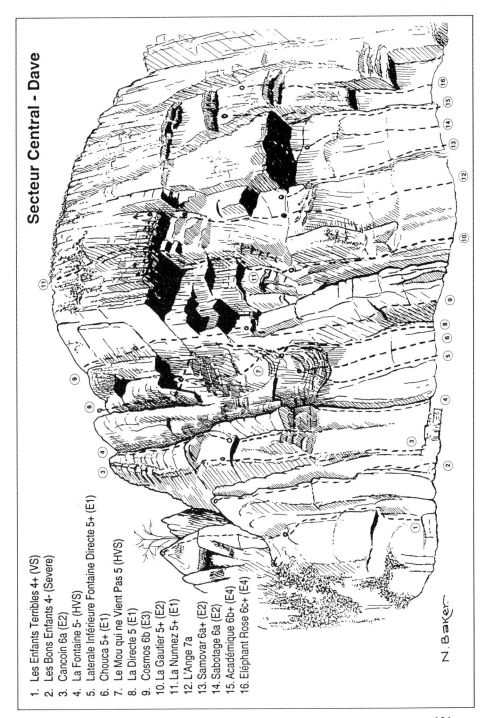

Secteur Central - Dave

1. Les Enfants Terribles 4+ (VS)
2. Les Bons Enfants 4- (Severe)
3. Cancoin 6a (E2)
4. La Fontaine 5- (HVS)
5. Laterale Inférieure Fontaine Directe 5+ (E1)
6. Chouca 5+ (E1)
7. Le Mou qui ne Vient Pas 5 (HVS)
8. La Directe 5 (E1)
9. Cosmos 6b (E3)
10. La Gautier 5+ (E2)
11. La Nunnez 5+ (E1)
12. L'Ange 7a
13. Samovar 6a+ (E2)
14. Sabotage 6a (E2)
15. Académique 6b+ (E4)
16. Eléphant Rose 6c+ (E4)

N. Baker

lies around to the right where adequate holds lead to the crest of the wall: good sport.

To the right of the foot of **LES AUTRICHIENS** is a deep chimney the right wall of which is formed by the small tower of the **BLOC DU PARACHUTE**. This contains three brief test pieces that are worth seeking out if you are into routes of a "short and hard" nature.

Turbo Cuisses * 6b (E3 6a) 40ft ◊
Start in the chimney and climb the leaning arête on the right until it is possible to pull onto a steeply inclined ramp on the left. Continue up the centre of the steep wall above.

Banane Pourrie 6c+ (E4 6b) 40ft ◊
Start as for the previous route but continue up the black-streaked leaning arête with considerable difficulty. Avoid the ledges on the right for the full effect.

Le Parachute 6a+ (E2 6a) 40ft ◊
Start at the left edge of the front of the tower and climb a groove and then the slabby front of the buttress to a flat ledge. From here climb the steep wall into the short hanging groove on the right. An action-packed few moves.

To the right is the easy descent gully containing the concrete pill-box and beyond this is another tower with prominent trees on its summit and copious vegetation on its left side. This is the **SECTEUR BONS ENFANTS** and again, as the name suggests, it contains a small selection of lower grade routes.

L'École 3 (V.Diff) 70ft ◊
A pleasant pitch with little fixed gear, perhaps a route to school you in preparation for a return to English ethics. A stepped overhang at 15ft is tackled direct by starting off a large block and is crossed on generous holds. Above this follow the slab to ledges.

Les Enfants Terribles ** 4+ (VS) 130ft P ◊
A good climb with an easy introduction leading to greater things. To the right of the overhang tackled by the previous route is a steep wide crack leading into an easier angled corner.
1. 70ft 3- (V.Diff) Avoid the initial wide crack by stepping in from the left off the block to reach a projecting ledge. Follow the crack line to a belay on the ledge above the finish of the previous climb.
2. 60ft 4+ (4c) Climb onto the highest ledge then head up the steep white slab to reach a short chimney and just a littler higher the summit of the tower.

To the right of the steep crack at the foot of the previous route is a left-facing corner. The next route climbs the narrow pillar between these two features.

L'Appendice 4+ (VS 4c) 70ft ◊
The initial section of the pillar is steep and tricky and then better holds are followed over a couple of minor bulges until below a section of steep imposing black rock. Here it is possible to traverse left around a corner and across to the stance at the top of the first pitch of **Les Enfants Terribles**. Finish up this or abseil off.

Just to the right is the steep left-facing corner mentioned above, with a triangular flake at its base. The corner leads up to a subsidiary tower below a steep wall high on the right. This is the initial pitch of

Les Bons Enfants ** 4- (Severe) 160ft
1. 80ft   4- (4a)   Start on the right arête of the corner and follow the long deep crack system up into a corner and over several bulges (always on good holds). A short distance above the last of these is a comfortable stance on top of this subsidiary buttress.

2. 80ft   3- (V.Diff) Climb over the top of the mini-tower and then descend to the base of a big corner that runs up to a col on the right. Pass below this to reach and follow the groove and chimney that lead to the large tree on the cliff top.

Above the stance at the top of the first pitch of **Les Bons Enfants** is a fine triangular wall that contains a couple of worthwhile pitches, though at the time of writing the bolts that protect them are rather old.

L'Ampezzane ** 5 (HVS 5a) 80ft
Spectacular climbing at a reasonable grade. From the stance climb to the highest point of the tower then trending rightwards up the wall to the prominent roof towards its top left corner. Pull leftwards over this then trend right to ledges and a substantial tree belay on top of the cliff.

La Cassin * 6a (E2 5c) 80ft
From the same stance below **L'Ampezzane** head rightwards up the bulging wall making for the obvious diagonal overlap high above. Climb this for a short distance until it is possible to pull leftwards across the roof on the steep head wall. Trend right from here to gain the arête, easy ground, and just a littler higher, the trees. It is probably best not to look down on this final section.

Around to the right is the next section of rock: the **SECTEUR FONTAINE - DIRECTE**. This is basically a steep pocketed slab capped by a bewildering set of overhangs and bounded on the right by the steep pocketed left-facing wall of **Cosmos**. The lower slab is riven by five marked cracks of varying widths. The first climb starts at the left edge of this area of rock at prominent twin blocks and almost

103

directly behind a prominent solitary tree. This is immediately to the right of the start of **Les Bons Enfants**.

L'Ancien Bleu * 4 (VS 4c) 90ft ◊

An enjoyable pitch that starts up the crack, passes a tricky bulge at 40ft and then trends left up the ramp below the steep wall tackled by the previous two routes to reach the stance on **Les Bons Enfants**. Abseil off or more logically finish up the top pitch of **Les Enfants Terribles** which can be approached by moving left after the short descent from the top of the tower (see above).

Cancoin ** 6a (E2) 190ft

A superb first pitch, though the second one is something of an anti-climax.

1. 100ft 6a (5c)   Climb the easy chimney-crack on the left side of the slab as for **L'Ancien Bleu** until just above its crux bulge. Here is possible to step right (painted arrow) to gain the arête. Up this steeply to a powerful couple of pulls over the crux roof. Small stance with lower offs just above the lip of the overhang.

2. 90ft 5 (5b)   A pitch with a touch of loose rock and some rather archaic protection; perhaps discretion is the better part of valour. Continue up the arête on the left to the next roof (pegs) and step onto the side wall which is climbed (peg and then bolts) until it is possible to pull back onto the slab on the right. Finish up this easily.

La Jefke ** 5- (HVS) 180ft

A pleasant outing that manages to sneak up steep rock without getting involved with anything too taxing.

1. 100ft 5- (4c)   Follow Cancoin until it steps right on to the arête. Step right again and climb the short steep wall (golos, that's hardly cricket) to gain a slab below a roof. Pull over this then belay on a small stance just to the right.

2. 80ft 3+ (Severe) Continue up the corner to pass the overhang by a crack on the right before following much easier terrain to the cliff top.

Altostratus ** 6c (E4 6a) 80ft ◊

Climb the white slab (name) to the right of the initial chimney-crack of the previous route to a section of much steeper rock. Have a breather then go for it, only the weak are spurned.

To the right a narrow crack (number 2 counting from the left) runs up to the left side of the central mass of overhangs and to the right of this is a similar but wider and deeper feature (number 3 counting from the left and the most prominent of the cracks). This is the first pitch of an ancient classic, first put up in 1934:

La Fontaine *** 5- (HVS) 170ft P

1. 50ft   4- (4b)   Climb the chimney through bulges to a cramped stance on the left (twin ring bolts) where it runs into steeper rock.

2. 40ft   5- (5a)   Make a gripping traverse 10ft to the left and haul into a large left-facing corner where a much-needed bridged rest is available. Climb this to a black roof and pull over to belay immediately.

3. 80ft   3+ (4a)   Continue up the corner and pass the bulge by a crack on the right before following easier "rock and two veg" to the cliff top.

To the right is crack line number 4:

Latérale Inferieure Fontaine Directe * 5+ (E1 5b) 80ft ◊

Climb the crack with the name Chouca until it starts to steepen dramatically then step right and pull up ever steepening rock to a couple of grasping moves over a sizable roof to a lowering point on the right: steep but generously equipped with "biffos".

At the point the route moves right it is possible to continue directly up the cliff following the impressive crack line to tick **Relax Pépère * 5+ (E2 5b)**.

Just to the right of the last climb is a steep slab tackle by the poor relative of a much more famous namesake.

Chouca * 5+ (E1 5b) 80ft ◊

Climb the pleasant slab to the right of the painted name to its top then continue up the bulging wall and over a small roof to a lowering point. If you had to do a dyno for a mono-doigt you are on the wrong route and in the wrong country.

Le Mou Qui Ne Vient Pas *** 5 (HVS 5a) 80ft ◊

A superb Vector-like pitch that weaves through the overhangs above the stance of the previous routes, space walking positions on bountiful holds. Approach by either of the previous two climbs or the rather easier (4c) first pitch of **La Directe** (see below).

Step right into the overhanging groove (as for **La Directe**) and climb this until it is possible to step out left onto a hanging slab. Climb this to a large roof which is crossed on the left using good finger holds to enter an easier corner. Up this to a another roof where a couple of moves left reach an exposed stance. Either abseil from here or, if you can't face that, finish up the top pitch of **La Directe 3 (Severe)** see below.

To the right the final crack in the lower slab starts a short distance left of the major corner line and runs up to meet it at the level of some large bulges. This is the line of another classic from the early 30s. Despite its name it isn't really all that direct!

La Directe ** 5 (E1) 200ft

1. 70ft   4- (4c)   Climb the crack line until it runs into the steep corner and then bridge up impending rock until it is possible to get back left to belay on a small exposed stance (the lowering point on **Chouca**).

2. 50ft   5 (5b)   Climb up right into an overhanging slot and bridge up this until it is possible to escape across the steep right wall (thread and peg) to more amenable rock. Saunter up to a smelly stance under a big roof or move left to a rather airier stance on the arête. A pitch which is quite gripping to lead, and very gripping to follow!

3. 80ft   3 (Severe)   Traverse left to outflank the overhangs then step round the corner and follow the easy groove to the cliff top.

To the right is a large left-facing and gently-leaning wall with a conspicuous band of overhangs cutting across it 30ft up. There are three good climbs here, though unfortunately the lower pitches are popular top rope problems and so are rather polished. They also tend to be greasy if the air is at all damp.

La Salaire de la Peur ** 6a (E2) 200ft P

1. 70ft   5 (4c) ◊   Climb the slabby corner on the left side of the wall (just to the right of the crack line of Pitch 1 of **La Directe**) to the roof. Pull rightwards over this then climb rightwards across the steep wall on a surprising set of holds to a good ledge at the apex of the wall.

2. 70ft   6a (5c)   Climb the steep corner behind the stance to a roof which is crossed by pulling rightwards to reach an exposed wall. Up this until an obvious traverse leads away right on the edge of all things (how can a pitch that looks so small from below look so big from up here?) and to a stance in a groove.

3. 60ft   3 (Severe)   Easy rock to the top.

Le Cosmos *** 6b (E3) 170ft

Excellent steep sustained climbing. The first pitch is often done on its own at beefy **(E2 5b) **.

1. 70ft   6a+ (5b) ◊ P   Start in the centre of the wall and climb steeply to the overhangs with a difficult move to reach them. Pull leftwards through these and continue up the middle of the wall by mildly pumpy climbing on generous jugs to the stance on top of the tower.

A right-hand variation to the central part of this pitch is a bit of a wimp out.

2. 100ft   6b (5c)   Climb up the steep corner to the roof and pull over its left edge. Continue up the superb sustained wall until it is possible to step into the corner on the left and an optional stance is reached. Abseil from here or follow "the garden path" above to the cliff top.

The ever-leaning wall of the first pitch of Le Cosmos, 6a+ (E2 5b), DAVE.
Climber: Nigel Baker

La Sommers * 6a (E1 5b) 70ft ◊ P

More pleasant hauling up gently tilted rock. Start 2m left of the right edge of the wall and climb slippery holds to the right edge of the roof. Continue until it is possible to pull right onto the arête. Either traverse right to a lowering point on a pillar or continue up the straightforward rib to the belays of the previous climb.

The cliff swings round to face west again and the slabby-looking lower wall is capped by some quite immense overhangs. Although many of the climbs go to the cliff top the lower pitches are far and away the most popular, especially as those in the centre rarely get wet. Many of the trees that used to shade the base of the wall have been cut down recently, so now it gets all the sun that is going.

The left side of this face is bounded by a rounded pillar with a chimney groove on its right. This pillar forms the right bounding arête of the previous three climbs, and is tackled directly by:

Tournevis * 5+ (HVS 5a) 60ft ◊
The left edge of the tower is followed throughout by staying on the sensible side.

Tache Cul * 5+ (E1 5b) 60ft ◊
The bolt ladder just to the right of the arête starts and finishes as for the previous route. The central section is a little steeper and rather less well endowed with holds.

The steep groove that bounds the pillar on its right side is the first pitch of the original route of the cliff put up by the grandly-named Xavier de Grunne in 1934. There is little doubt that the equipment used was rudimentary and that the climb was a serious undertaking all those years ago. It rather puts the development of UK limestone climbing of the same era in perspective. This early adventure is:

La Grunne ** 5 (E1) 270ft
A good climb that is rather spoilt by the out of character nature of the crux moves. The use of an aid point here would reduce the climb to **(VS 4c)** and increase its star rating to an exciting *** expedition to some wild places.

1. 60ft 4 (4b) ◊ Climb the rather polished twinned chimney-groove to a belay on a ledge at its top.

2. 40ft 3 (Severe) ◊ Trend left up the obvious line to a small stance in a corner on "the edge of all things".

3. 50ft 5 (5b) Climb the corner to the roof then move left onto the exposed arête. Cross the wall leftwards to reach the hanging slab by a perplexing couple of moves (if you are really perplexed or find the exposure a bit much, try swinging on the bolt) then climb the slab to an odious stance below even bigger overhangs. At this point you may be starting to wonder how you got into this mess!

4. 120ft 3 (Severe) Move left and up to the roof before stepping round the exposed corner to arrive at much easier terrain (possible stance) and once composure is restored continue easily to the top. Perhaps long routes are fun after all.

La Nunnez ** 5+ (E1) 140ft (210ft from the ground)

Starting from the lowering point at the top of the first pitch of the previous route is this great little exercise in space walking. Combining this with **Gautier** (see below) gives a distinguished *** trip up the cliff.

1. 70ft 5b ◊ Step right from the stance and climb over a small roof into a cramped corner. Lay-back round the next roof and continue past a third one (the downward view gets ever more exciting) to a hanging corner under the biggest of the overhangs. Either move left to a lowering point or traverse out right to a stance just above the lip.

2. 70ft 3 (Severe) The easy groove leads to the cliff top.

La Gautier ** 5+ (E2 5c) 70ft ◊

In the right wall of the open groove of **Le Grunne** is a shallow yellow sentry box below an open groove. This is approached from directly below and gives a surprising pitch being alternately fingery and precarious, with the bolts being almost "sportingly" placed. Lower off or move left and continue up **La Nunnez** (see above) for a *** trip to the cliff top.

Magic Fly *** 7a 80ft ◊

Starting from the belay above **Gautier** is something a little more challenging. Step right and climb the awkward leaning groove in the arête and pull over onto (marginally) easier angled rock. Continue up and right over an exhausting series of bulges and roofs, with the final trio being the icing on the cake. Above the final large overhang is a lowering point above the lip of the last roof on **La Nunnez**, a pitch whose angle only becomes really apparent when you lower off.

Strato Nimbus ** 6a+ (E2 6a) 70ft ◊

The bulging rounded rib which separates the open grooves of **La Grunne** and **Jomouton** gives a good butch pitch with mixed messages. The good news is that all the holds are in the form of excellent incuts, the bad news is that unfortunately some of them are rather small! 3 bolts protect rather sportingly.

Jomouton * 6a+ (E3)

An wandering and rather unbalanced route with a tough crux and very exposed stance as well as a lot of easier climbing. The first pitch is well worthwhile on its own as a pleasant, if sheepish, introduction to this section of cliff at * **4+ (VS 4c)**.

1. 70ft 4+ (4c) ◊Climb the slab into a straightforward groove on the right-side of the rounded pillar (take care not to confuse this with the chimney-groove of La Grunne 10ft further left) until it steepens and a couple of harder moves can be made to a tiny stance on the right. Lower off or

2. 70ft 6a+ (6a) Traverse right along the weakness passing some very substantial runners to the obvious hanging corner which is climbed to the huge overhang. Traverse right under this and pull over the lip to belay immediately.

3. 80ft 3 (Severe) Climb around the corner on the left to a slab which is followed into an easy finishing chimney.

Globules *** 7a 160ft

Immediately to the right of the easy corner of **Jomouton** is a pale slab leading to a steep wall and a prominent line of small roofs at 50ft. There are four routes over these, with two of them pressing on up the much more imposing bulges above.

1. 70ft 5+ (E2 5c) ◊ Climb straight up the wall passing just to the left of the overhangs to a constricted stance. A worthwhile pitch in its own right, **(*)**.

2. 90ft 7a ◊ Climb straight up the steep wall to the centre of the big black double roof above, and cross this gymnastically to a rest below a bigger roof (possible lowering point). Do battle with this and then swing right to the lowering point in a corner. Impressive stuff requiring big arms.

L'Ange *** 7a 160ft

Another stamina route with a worthwhile first pitch **(**)** even if you are not up to the taxing second one.

1. 70ft 6a+ (E3 6a) ◊ Start under the left edge of the overhang at 50ft and climb directly to and through it to a small stance.

2. 90ft 7a ◊ Head up the wall into the large hanging corner and over a series of sizable overhangs. The holds are generous but the angle is a mite excessive throughout: brilliant but not a route for suffers of vertigo.

For those who prefer their sport a little nearer the ground there is a right-hand finish to the first pitch, **Contre-Temps 7a+ ** 70ft** ◊, which only has 15ft of independent climbing but it really packs it in, get laybacking!

Caméléon *** 7a 120ft

Another action packed trip through impressive territory. Start below the right side of the small overhang at 50ft.

1. 70ft 7a ◊ Climb the steep wall to the bulges which are tackled direct and prove to be problematical, a great piece of pocket pulling. A small stance and big ring is reached just above the bulges.

2. 50ft 6b ◊ Climb the corner on the right (part of **La Jomouton**) to below the huge roof, and when suitably inspired, go for it. The holds are generally huge, but then again they need to be!

It is possible to run the two pitches together, in which case you can award yourself a big **7a+ ***** tick.

To the right is the largest overhang on the crag, hanging in space 70ft off the ground. There are five worthwhile routes on the wall below the overhang and two that actually cross it. The great roof makes the wall below appear slabby; rest assured it is not, as your forearms will soon confirm. ·

Samovar ** 6a+ (E2 5c) 80ft ◊

Start directly under the left edge of the impressive overhang and climb the wall passing a much smaller roof en route to a poor rest in the groove below the roof by a lowering ring (lowering from here reduces the route to **6a (E2 5b) ****. Climb up to the roof and exit awkwardly leftwards on good but spaced holds to a lowering point in the corner above. If you have not had enough a logical extension from here is the upper half of **Jomouton 6a+ (E3 6a)**.

The next four climbs all end up at a cluster of substantial lowering points under the centre of the great overhang, with the prominent line of bolt-on holds across it!

La Rotule * 5+ (E1 5b) 70ft ◊
Start up a left-slanting crack and move right to follow the leftmost bolt line that runs up to the big overhang, passing around the left edge of a small overhang on the way, and with a final tricky move to the belays.

Rêve ** 5+ (E2 5c) 70ft ◊
Start off as for the previous route but move further right to cross the centre of the band of small overhangs by sustained and fingery moves.

Sabotage ** 6a (E2 5b) 70ft ◊
Possibly the best of the bunch on this lower wall. Begin below a stepped groove in the small band of overhangs at 50ft and climb up to the right edge of the groove. A series of blind moves are made up and left to reach easier angled rock and then the rings.

Exorcist ** 6a+ (E2 5c) 80ft ◊
A climb with a good lower and middle section leading to a rather illogical finish. Start below the right side of the big overhangs under a prominent twin roof at 50ft. Climb straight up to the lower roof then powerful moves lead up steep rock to the lip of the second overhang. Swing awkwardly left to join the final few moves of the previous climb.

Above the lowering point for the last four pitches is a most bizarre piece of climbing, best suited to chimpanzees or climbers who have spent the last 6 months in the Foundry:

Surprise Sur Prise *** 6b+ (E3 5c) 30ft ◊
The line of bolt on holds are followed across the 20ft ceiling to a lowering point just around the lip, head for the ground. One natural hold may have to be used if you don't plan ahead. A gripping pitch to lead and a very gripping pitch to follow, especially with your belayer safely back on the deck!

The other line across the overhang is a whole different ball game:

Le Pen * 7c 30ft ◊
The right-hand line has good protection and hardly any holds, possibly the hardest pitch on the cliff at present.

Académique *** 6b+ (E4 6a) 90ft ◊

The groove that skirts the right side of the great roof is very worthwhile though some of the rock is rather odd.

Climb into the groove and follow it steeply by sustained moves to a rest below the overhang that blocks access into the continuation directly above. Large holds lead through this to a pair of golos that protect!!! the crux pull into the upper groove (obviously strenuous) then follow easier rock to a lowering point on the right. It is possible to press on easily to the cliff top though this is not a very edifying experience!

To the right of the groove that leads to the right side of the great overhang is an area of steeply leaning rock that has an excellent collection of climbs, well suited to those who like to "pump it up".

Cacadémique *** 7a 90ft ◊

A superb pitch that leans forever then leans a bit more!

Climb the steep wall to the right of the long crack of the previous route and pull up into a niche with difficulty (the technical crux?), then do battle with the never-ending series of bulges above. A semi-detached block (surely it must be solid!!) is used to gain a shallow corner that leads more easily to the lowering point. At the risk of being repetitive I will say it again, quite simply: superb.

Éléphant Rose *** 6c+ (E4 6a) ◊

Marginally easier but just as magnificent as its near neighbour, with holds that are just as good and resting places that are a little better.

Climb a ragged crack and then a short leaning wall steeply (often a bit greasy) into a roofed-in corner where a bridged rest is available. Exit rightwards from here and continue over two sizable overhangs on generous holds (well except for on the second one) to the lowering anchors. Steep with a capital "st".

The impressive series of bulges to the right of the roofed in corner of **Éléphant Rose** are crossed by two of the cliff's hardest offerings.

Spoutnic ** 7b+ 60ft ◊

Start as for the previous climb but at 20ft move right into a corner. Cross the roof with great difficulty and continue up the groove above to the lowering station.

Kangourou * 7c 60ft ◊

A route with a savage crux sequence which crosses the trio of pocketed overhangs on the right side of the wall using a series of stuck-on pebbles (now there's an interesting solution to blank rock). If you flash this one there is not much else on the cliff that will entertain you!

To the right is a projecting buttress with ledges at 20ft that are reached by scrambling around to the right. This is the **SECTEUR SUPER VOL ET YETI**. The climbs here are generally short but are quite worthwhile, perhaps a suitable venue if the central section of cliff is busy. The buttress is basically a short wall capped by block overhangs and split by a steep groove. The first route starts from the left end of the ledge, by a painted bomb, and heads away left through impressive territory at a reasonable grade, always a sure-fire recipe for a classic.

La Pierlot *** 5 (E1) 240ft

1. 100ft 5 (5b)   Climb the rib on the left into a crack until the rock begins to lean then continue left to a rest on a block. From here it is possible to trend left following a line of weakness through the bulges eventually to gain a steep groove. There is a belay and stance 30ft up this. Your second will doubtless describe this pitch as **HVS 5a** but then he would, wouldn't he?

2. 140ft 3 (Severe) Climb through the overhang and follow the long chimney line to the cliff top, or abseil from the stance.

Starting in the same place (by the painted bomb) but heading straight up the leaning wall is:

Cric Crac Boum * 6c (E4 6a) 50ft ◊

Climb the lower wall then power through the bulge on mostly good (who says they are chipped?) holds to gain easier rock on the left. Up and right to a lower off.

Les Ventouses * 6c (E4 6a) 50ft ◊

Climb the thin wall to the left of the central chimney to reach the large roof at twin bolts (always a bad sign). Cross this dramatically (6c on the left, 6c+ centrally) to reach the belays.

The groove that splits the overhangs above the right side of the starting ledge is gained by a steep initial wall and is;

Super Vol * 5+ (E1 5b) 40ft ◊

Climb the tricky wall to gain the groove and climb through the overhangs by contortionistic bridging to reach belays on the left just around the lip.

Just to the right the other half of the buttress has a slabby lower wall capped by a series of bulges. Once again there are some short but worthwhile pitches here. Starting at the toe of the buttress is

Super Pili-Pili ** 5- (VS 4c) 60ft P ◊

Climb slabby rock leftwards to gain the arête and follow this to below the omnipresent overhangs. Pull right then back leftwards through these on massive holds to gain a steep wall which is followed on good holds to the crest of the buttress.

Yeti * 5+ (E1 5b) 60ft P ◊

Start as for the last route but climb straight up the initial slab to a narrow overhang which is crossed on the right. Follow the corner to the capping roof then step left (an exit to the right is easy but you can't tick the route if you take it) and climb the leaning groove by an abominable move to the cliff top.

The steep wall that bounds the initial slab of the previous two routes is climbed centrally by;

Amazone * 5 (HVS 5a) 50ft ◊

The middle of the wall is followed throughout on a fine selection of holds to a final tricky pull rightwards onto the arête. Continue to the top of the tower. Not quite the ferocious man-eater that the name suggests.

Around the corner to the right is the

Chimnée du Bivouac ** 3 (V.Diff) 50ft P ◊

The slanting break with a slabby left wall is a great beginner's pitch, leading to a spacious platform. From its top a free abseil over the roofs of the **SECTEUR YETI** is an exciting way back to the ground.

Above and right of the **SECTEUR YETI** is a bay with a steep north-facing wall, the secluded **SECTEUR LOULOU** rising above the Platforme du Bivouac. This area is most easily reached by the **Cheminée du Bivouac** (see above). It can also be reached from the top of any of the routes on the **SECTEUR SUPER VOL ET YETI**. Either access route leads to a broad terrace. At the back left side of this of this is a large slab, well hidden from below:

L'Ovni * 5 (VS 5a) 50ft P ◊

The slab gives a sustained piece of climbing, worth the effort involved in getting at it. Start on the left and pull through the bulges, or start more easily from the right. Continue up the sustained slab past several peg runners to a tree belay. Abseil off.

The right side of the terrace has a steep wall with a small selection of pitches that could do with rebolting.

Jardin Noir 5+ (E2 5b) 50ft ◊

Climb a short distance up the chimney crack (apparently a classical caving trip, though I managed to refrain from checking it out) that bounds the left side of the wall until it is possible to head directly up the face by steep and sustained moves; not overly protected.

Les Valseuses * 5+ (E2 5c) 60ft ◊

Start at the foot of the chimney on the left side of the wall and climb up to a ledge by fingery and sustained moves, from where a short crack is followed up and right. From the top of this finish directly up the wall. Again more a sporting route than a sport route.

The right side of the wall has a prominent small roof at 30ft and just left of this is a steep flake crack:

La Loulou 5 (HVS 5a) 40ft ◊

The crack is followed to a belay on a ledge system, surprisingly strenuous.

To the right is a deep bulging chimney, the line of

L'Érotique * 4+ (VS 4c) 80ft P

The chimney offers a pleasant pitch, quite steep and intimidating though not quite as titillating as the name suggests.

To the right of the start of **La Loulou** a narrow ledge runs out to the right. A cemented ring here offers an good anchor point for a straightforward abseil back to the ground.

The penultimate buttress is generally rather vegetated though there are a couple of worthwhile low grade climbs that thread their way through the cabbages.

La Merveilleuse ** 3 (V.Diff) 140ft

The long deep chimney on the right of the **Cheminée du Bivouac** gives a remarkably pleasant climb, with its enclosed nature making it ideal for timid beginners. It is normal to split the route with a belay at 60ft though it can be done in one rope length.

50 metres to the right is

Wassland ** 3+ (Severe) 160ft

Another long low grade route that appears rather vegetated from below but is well worth doing; try to keep to the clean rock! Start at the right edge of a slab to the right of a roofed-in corner.

1. 70ft 3- (V.Diff) Climb the slab trending left to pass above the lip of the overhang. A comfortable stance is reached just before an arête.

2. 90ft 3+ (Severe) Climb straight up the fine sustained slab, passing a small overhang just above the stance and one just below the cliff top, exit rightwards.

Further right is the final section of cliff, the petite **SECTEUR JET 27** characterised by a series of three block overhangs. There are about ten short climbs here across a range of grades and the place is probably best left until you have done everything else on the cliff. For completeness the main lines are from left to right (fill in your own star ratings and UK grades):

Météorite 6c The left line over the first roof.

Magique Noire 6b+ The right line over the same.

Axe 24 5 The line that weaves up the left arête of the central overhang.

Jet 27 6b The middle of the central roof.

Spit Bazar 4+ The chimney to the right of the central roof.

Codo 6b+ The line through the left side of the right-hand series of roofs.

Les Buveurs Volants 7a+ The line through the centre of the right-hand roof.

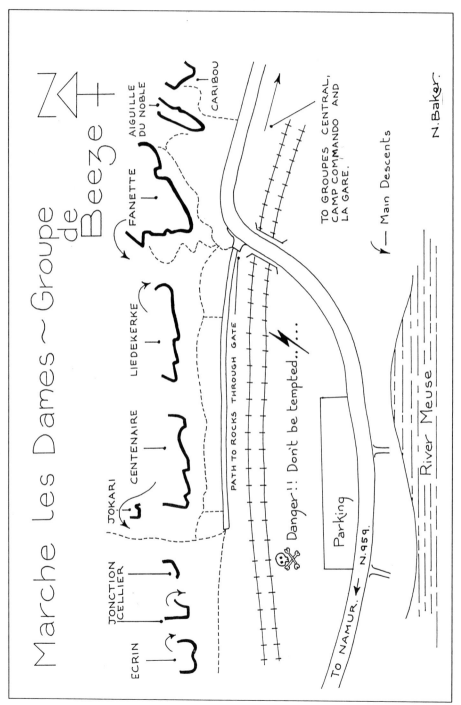

Marche Les Dames ~ Groupe de Beeze

N. Baker.

ECRIN
JONCTION CELLIER
JOKARI
CENTENAIRE
LIEDEKERKE
FANETTE
AIGUILLE DU NOBLE
CARIBOU

PATH TO ROCKS THROUGH GATE

Danger!! Don't be tempted......

Parking

TO NAMUR.
N.959.

TO GROUPES CENTRAL, CAMP COMMANDO AND LA GARE.

— Main Descents

River Meuse

MARCHE LES DAMES

INTRODUCTION

The cliffs at Marche les Dames are amongst the most extensive in Belgium. Rising from the wooded banks of the Meuse valley there are twenty-three individually defined buttresses up to 200 feet high that run in a line above the road and railway line for three kilometres. At present there are over 400 routes here, only minutes from the road, and varying in grade from 2 to 8a. Almost all are superbly equipped with big multi-coloured bolts, and substantial belays/lower offs, all courtesy of the Belgian Alpine Club.

There are occasional patches of soft rock and some of the buttresses tend to be rather vegetated, though this is the exception rather than the rule. The bases of some of the cliffs are quite close to the road and the railway line so it can be fairly noisy on occasions, though the trees cut out much of the sound. In summer it can get oppressively hot here but then again that makes a nice change!

Basically the cliffs are divided into four main sections, from west to east these are the **Groupe de Beez**, the **Groupe Central**, the **Camp Commando**, and the **Groupe de Gare**. Unfortunately three of the four areas at **MARCHE LES DAMES** have limited access at the moment, for a variety of reasons.

The **Group Central** has been closed for some years as large sections of it tower over the road, the risk of falling rocks landing on the road is a very real one. The **Camp Commando**, as the name suggests rises straight from the grounds of the Belgian Commandos training camp (perhaps it is best not to wear your floral lycra if you climb here!). Access to the cliffs is restricted to weekends and holidays and you are supposed to report to the guards post and leave your alpine club card and another means of identification with the guard. In reality most Belgians ignore this rule and just climb over the fence to get at the cliffs, how well do you think you can blend in?

The superb and extensive **Groupe de Gare** has recently been closed because of problems with the residents who live in front of the cliffs. The eventual outcome here is still uncertain, check the situation locally.

Despite these closures all is not lost as the **Groupe de Beez** has over 200 routes on nine separate buttresses to go at, enough to keep most people happy for a day or two.

GEOGRAPHY

The **GROUPE DE BEEZ** is the first section of cliff reached on the approach from Namur and it consists of nine separate buttresses. On the far left is the **ROCHER DE L'ÉCRIN** with its conspicuous central cave/arch. To the right of this and set back slightly is the very popular **ROCHER DE LA JONCTION**.

Behind the **ROCHER DE LA JONCTION** is a pleasant wooded valley containing two small buttresses, the flat wall of the **ROCHER DU CELLIER** on the left and the overhanging block of the **SURPLOMB JOKARI** on the right. The next buttress is the extensive **ROCHER DU CENTENAIRE** directly in front of the centre of the parking place, with a vegetated central section and an easy ramp line rising across its left-hand side. Right again is another large and complex buttress the **ROCHER DE LIEDEKERKE**, just west of the railway bridge. Almost directly above this bridge is the **ROCHER DE LA FANETTE** which is characterised by an impressive square tower on it left side. The final sections of rock are **THE AIGUILLES DU NOBLE** and **ROCHER CARIBOU** protruding from the trees above the railway bridge.

The buttresses are described from left to right, many routes have their names painted at their base, and many of the bolt lines are colour coded.

APPROACHES

The cliffs overlook the north bank of River Meuse and the N959 between the small towns of Beez and Marche les Dames, six kilometres east of Namur. There is an extensive parking area in front of the central section of the cliff. Walk eastwards along the road, over a railway bridge then turn sharp left through a gate to reach the narrow overgrown track that runs back below the cliffs. The direct route from the car park to the cliffs should be avoided, if you are considering ignoring the warning signs, the speed the trains pass should make you think again!

ROCHER DE L'ÉCRIN

The left-most worthwhile piece of rock is this 90ft high buttress which is riven centrally by a cave/arch. All the climbs are exceptionally well equipped and can be done to the belays and back to the ground on a 45m rope.

To the left of the arch is a flat wall with a band of small overhangs which are stepped on their left side, three-quarters of the way up the cliff.

Le Temps des Secrets * 5 (HVS 5a) 60ft ◊

The left-most route on the cliff starts up a shallow corner and finishes over a small overhang, a pleasant introduction to the cliff at an amenable grade.

Risques Éperdus ** 7a 70ft ◊

The left arête of the front face of the buttress is climbed via the right edge of the prominent white streak to a position below the big roof at the top left corner of the face. This is crossed on the left or right with some difficulty,

Les Fils du Deuxième Millénaire *** 6a (E2 5c) 70ft ◊

Climb the centre of the face to ledges below the obvious break in the bulges. Climb through these powerfully then trend slightly right to the top. A great pitch and somewhat steeper than it appears from below.

Unis Vers L'Uni ** 6b+ (E4 6a) 70ft ◊
The bulge to the right of the previous route is approached directly and climbed by an unhelpful series of pockets, distinctly uphill work.

L'Arête de Boisson ** 4 (VS 4b) 80ft ◊
The right arête of the face (and the left edge of the cave) offers pleasant climbing at a much more reasonable grade than the routes further left. Climb the front face (tricky move at 30ft) or the steep pocketed crack in the arête to ledges. Step right then follow the right side of the arête in excellent position and on good holds to a lower off on top of the buttress.

To the right is the central cave that roughly splits the buttress in two. There is a 5+ round the left side of the overhangs and a 6c directly over the roof of the cave, though the next route described takes the groove that passes to the right of the overhangs:

Exultate Jubilate ** 5+ (E1 5b) 70ft ◊
A worthwhile pitch up the twisting groove line but not perhaps quite as good as the name suggests! Climb the wall to the right edge of the overhangs and pull into the corner. Follow it with sustained interest, mostly by jamming and bridging.

The right wall of the cave recess has a bulging groove with steep black left wall:

On Ne Peut Pas Être Et Avoir Été ** 6b (E3 6a) 70ft ◊
Easy rock leads to the base of the groove which gives fine sustained climbing with a big feel for such a small cliff.

Je ne suis pas dans le Gris par Accident ** 6a (E3 6a) 60ft ◊
The wall to the right of the big groove gives a sustained and fingery piece of climbing, no sneaking off to the right at the top!

Demain J'Enlève Le Haut ** 6b (E3 6a) 70ft ◊
The left arête of the right-hand section of cliff gives a good sustained pitch, particularly tough on the upper reaches where the route climbs the centre of the hanging shield. The blue dotted lines are to ensure you don't stray too far from the straight and narrow!

L'Arc De Sebastien ** 5 (E1 5b) 70ft ◊
Start to the right of the arête and climb through a bulge on good holds to reach a hanging flake. Pull leftwards over this and romp on to the top.

Le Makitova Ne Repond Plus ** 4+ (HVS 5a) 60ft P ◊
The crack that splits the centre of the right-hand buttress is tougher than it looks being both steep and polished, a pumpy combination. Try to blast up the lower

119

section because the upper half is much easier.

Le Matin Des Braves * 5 (HVS 5a) 40ft ◊
The bulge to the right of the central crack has good holds, but they are spaced and the route is a touch steep.

LE ROCHER DE LA JONCTION
The next buttress to the right is set back slightly and is no more than 60ft high. It has a long left-hand face where the routes tend to be rather crowded together and somewhat steep, and a narrower front face set at a more reasonable angle. The routes are well equipped and this, added to the fact that there are several climbs in the lower grades, makes it an ideal venue for beginners or newcomers to sport climbing. The whole buttress is always popular. On the down-side, though not surprisingly, many of the climbs are rather polished. The routes are described from left to right.

The left side of the face has a prominent bulge cutting across it at mid height. There are five rather cramped ways over the bulge all protected by substantial cemented pegs. Do them all for a good work out.

In Vino Veritas 5- (VS 5a) 30ft ◊
The groove at the left edge of the cliff leads to and through the bulge.

Mets Tes Mains Sur La Table * 5 (HVS 5a) 30ft ◊
Follow the white streak to and through the white bulges above.

Sex Traction * 5- (VS 4c) 30ft ◊
The obvious rift in the bulges offers an easy way through for those with big arms, lesser mortals might puff a bit.

Beez Poursuite 5 (HVS 5a) 40ft ◊
Start at the painted name and climb straight up the wall to the roof, pull through it using the right side of the big hole. Press on more easily to the belays.

V.D.Q.S. ** 5+ (E1 5b) 40ft ◊
Start below the hole containing inconspicuous chains and climb the leaning wall to reach them, continue through the bulge above this substantial runner.

To the right are two deep chimney cracks both of which offer good low grade climbs.

Moi, Je Fais de la Montagne ** 3 (V.Diff) 50ft ◊
The left-hand chimney crack is approached up a straightforward juggy wall and gives pleasant bridging.

L'Hortisculpteur ** 4- (Severe) 50ft ◊

The right-hand crack with its prominent jammed block is also well worth doing and is protected by "gert big bolts".

Immediately to the right of the right-hand crack are two climbs up a steep wall.

Beezodrome * 5 (HVS 5a) 50ft ◊

Follow the left-hand line (red bolts) which is steep and sustained and has a tricky bulge thrown in for good measure.

A2 C'est Mieux * 5 (HVS 5a) 50ft ◊

The right-hand line has pretty blue bolts. Start up a groove then follow steeper rock to the lower offs.

To the right is a right-trending overlap springing from a hole. Starting under the left edge of this is:

Pelomaniaque ** 5 (HVS 5a) 60ft ◊

The best route of its grade on this face (red bolts). Pull over the left edge of the overhang to gain the wall and follow the front of the pillar above to the top.

Beau Mâle Fuscia * 5+ (E1 5b) 60ft ◊

This route follows the line of spaced blue bolts, very butch. Climb to the right edge of the overlap and pull awkwardly into the groove that rises from its right edge. Follow this with interest to the belays.

Masculino Ma Non Fanatico ** 6a (E2 5c) 60ft ◊

The final offering before the cliff swings round is a great pitch. Climb through the initial bulge to gain the wall and climb this on mostly good holds, first left then right. The red bolts on this one are almost too close together.

The next routes are on the narrower front face of the tower which is split by a central groove and capped by a prominent tree on its right side. The rock here is not too steep and there is an excellent collection of climbs facing the railway line, make sure you wave to the passers by.

Inoxis * 4+ (VS 5a) 60ft ◊

The first line of fixed gear right of the arête is a blue one. Follow this (initially past a peg), over a couple of bulges on excellent holds, easing as height is gained. From the ledge continue up the slab.

Manetball * 4 (VS 4b 60ft ◊

Follow the red bolts up the steep slab to the right to a ledge and possible stance. Continue up steeper rock to the top.

Evline * 5- (VS 4c) 60ft ◊

The arête just left of the central groove gives a pleasant pitch. Above the ledge a tricky slab leads to the belays.

Balade Nocturne ** 4 (Severe 4a) 60ft ◊

The central groove offers a good sustained pitch, which is quite steep towards the top. The name suggests that the route should be done at night, it this Belgium's answer to **Lockwood's Chimney?**

Crocodile Dundee * 5 (HVS 5a) 60ft ◊

You've seen the film, now try the route. Start just to the right of the central groove and climb the white face (peg runners) to pass a small hanging flake to arrive at the tree.

This final section is the crux, though it can be avoided by moving right (4c).

Femelle Aligote * 4 (VS 4b) 60ft ◊

The sustained slab to the right is followed without deviation past red bolts and a crack line.

Li Roayeu de Cruau * 4 (VS 4b) 60ft ◊

The right arête of the front face is followed past blue bolts.

The right-hand side of the cliff is narrow and steep. There is a trio of routes here the best of which is the left one starting at a tree stump;

La Grande Brune ** 4+ (VS 4c) 50ft ◊

From the stump follow a crack into a deeper groove which leads steeply to the top. A pitch well protected by substantial stainless steep loops.

The two steep lines to the right pass either side of the hanging block. They are of a similar grade to the previous route but of lesser quality.

En Un État Douteux * 4+ (VS 4c) 50ft ◊

The left-hand line.

L'Informateur De La Presse * 4+ (VS 4c) 50ft ◊

No prizes for guessing where this one goes.

To the right of **LE ROCHER DE LA JONCTION** is a shallow wooded valley with two small outcrops in it. On the left side is the flat wall of **ROCHER DU CELLIER** which has a small collection of fairly scruffy face routes. Across on the other side of the valley is the small prominent block overhang of the **SURPLOMB JOKARI**. This piece of rock is worth a visit just to see how many bolts you can get in one piece of rock! It is obvious that someone has been on a mission here, it is a wonder the amount of metal work in the rock doesn't cause the buttress to tip over. For completeness the eight routes here are described briefly, it is certainly a good place to get the route tally for the holiday up a bit. A little blinkering is needed or you might end up getting two ticks in one go.

Comteur a Gase 5+ (E1 5b) 20ft ◊

The small overhang/cave at the left side of the cliff provides the substance of this rather dirty offering, yellow bolts mark the line.

Les Fiasques de Chianti 5 (HVS 5a) 20ft ◊

Start off a block and follow the blue bolts on good holds up rapidly easing rock.

La Dalle des Gros Bras 5 (HVS 5a) 20ft ◊

Climb the steep wall (red bolts) past the hanging, but well cemented flake. The name means "the wall of big arms" and not anything else you might misconstrue.

Tétanisation * 5+ (E1 5b) 30ft ◊

The groove towards the right side of the left face is steep and the holds though good are well spaced, blue bolts.

Nazareth by Night 6a (E2 5c) 30ft ◊

The arête is followed as direct as possible past yellow bolts.

Le Surplomb Jokari * 6a (E2 5c) 30ft ◊

The "original and best" outing on this section of rock. The front face is climb slightly rightwards on good but well spaced holds. If the route went on much further it would be a real classic.

Le Toit des Gringalets 6b (E2 5c) 30ft ◊

The right arête of the wall is climbed on huge holds, pity they are so far apart.

The next piece of rock to the right is the extensive **ROCHER DU CENTENAIRE**, originally named by the developers in honour of the centenary of the Belgian Alpine Club.

The cliff is the broad face opposite the centre of the car parking space. It is split to the left of centre by a huge corner system and to the right of this the central area of the cliff is a vegetated area of rock. To the left of the corner an easy ramp rises rightwards across the face to join the final section of the corner. Above this ramp a series of conspicuous stepped overhangs cut across the face, several tough routes battle their way round these. To the right of the big corner is a broad face with a gargantuan fallen flake below its centre. The majority of the routes described here are towards the left side of the cliff.

Descent: Either abseil back down the line of the route if it is suitably equipped (some of the cliff top trees have wire cables for this purpose) or walk back into the wood to pick up a path that descends into the valley to the left of the cliff.

The left side of the face has a prominent easy ramp cutting across it from left to right. At the foot of this is a cave directly above which is a steep shallow corner **(La Bibiche)** running straight up the cliff. Left of this is a series of blocky ledges at 15ft and left again is a easy rib which is the starting point for five routes of which the best two are described here.

The Sound of Silence ** 5+ (E1 5b) 100ft
Start 15ft left of the cave and climb the easy wall heading for the steep groove high above (red bolts). Enter the groove and follow it impressively to the cliff top.

Bananarama *** 5+ (E2 5c) 100ft
Start just right of the previous route but at the second bolt trend right to enter a long shallow groove (blue bolts). Follow this, steep and fingery to a swing right near its top, and then continue up the wall above more easily.

La Bibiche *** 5- (HVS 4c) 110ft
A long sustained and classical pitch up the long corner system above the cave. Climb onto a large sloping ledge from the groove on the left and move right to below the corner. Enter it steeply and continue without deviation to the cliff top.

La Caroline *** 5 (HVS 5a) 150ft
Another "big" route at an amenable grade. Start just to the left of cave at the foot of the easy ramp that cuts across the impressive face to the right.
   1. 100ft 5 (5a)   Climb the steep leaning wall 3ft left of the cave to ledges (no bridging back to the opposite wall at the start) and then move right and climb the centre of the bulging wall aiming for the roof high on the right. A small stance is available in the short groove below the roof.
   2. 50ft 4 (4b)   Climb to the roof then move out right in an exposed situation to reach easy ground.
      A direct finish moving left then right through the bulges directly above the stance on good holds is also possible at 5 (5a) if you want a touch more excitement.

Le Escalator ** 2 (Diff) 200ft
The easy ramp that runs across the face offers access to several routes on the steep upper wall. It is also a worthwhile trip for beginners through impressive surroundings.
   Start 6ft right of the cave and spiral up easy rock to the right before following the front of the buttress to a belay at the lower end of the ramp. Follow the ramp

The fingery crux of Bananarama, 5+ (E2 5c), ROCHER DU CENTENAIRE, MARCHE LES DAMES. Climber: Andy Watts

up and right (gripping upward views) to a belay above the big corner system on the right. Finish up the easy open groove to the cliff top.

The wall that towers above the ramp of **Le Escalator** contains seven routes, most of which are tough. Three of the best routes are described here, though if you enjoy the "out there" setting there are others to do.

Genesis ** 5+ (E2 5b) 70ft

Sustained and enjoyable climbing up the left edge of the upper wall. From the stance at the bottom of the ramp on **Le Escalator** climb the wall trending slightly leftwards by sustained moves until it is possible to step left round the arête and join **La Caroline** to finish.

La Machine à Rodolphe *** 6b (E4) 160ft

A classic diagonal line across the cliff.

1. 60ft 5+ (5b)   Start as for **Genesis** and at the third bolt traverse horizontally to the right to the left edge of the overhangs, then continue in the same line to a hanging stance under the roofs on some big red bolts.

2. 100ft 6b (6a)   Climb round the right edge of the overlap into a recess then undercut out to the right to eventually reach a cramped rest in a niche. Exit from the right side of this via a crack containing a large hole and press on to the top, what a pumper!

La Polytechnique ** 6c (E4 6a) 80ft

From the stance at the bottom of the ramp on **Le Escalator** trend right then climb straight up the wall to the left end of the obvious overhangs. Either traverse 10ft right to a hanging stance on the prominent red bolts, or press on round the left edge of the roof and up the crack above.

Below and to the right of the ramp of **Le Escalator** and 30ft right of the cave at the foot of the cliff is a large triangular wall containing two worthwhile routes (that could do with being rebolted), and bounded on the right by a steep corner.

Le Pilier du Centenaire * 5+ (E1 5b) 100ft

The left-hand line is followed easily to a ramp system that leads up and right to a resting ledge. Pull into the steep crack above and follow this to a belay at the top of the ramp on **Escalator**. Abseil from here or climb the easy groove on the right to the cliff top.

L'Exaltante *** 5+ (E3) 170ft

A great route that would only be E2 if it was properly bolted. As it stands the crux wall is a touch worrying!

1. 100ft 5+ (5c)   Steady climbing leads straight up the centre of the wall to below a more imposing section. Pull past a small overhang then press on up the steep sustained wall to the stance on the previous climb.

2. 70ft 5 (5a)   Abseil off or climb into the leaning crack on the left to an exposed exit into a crack which leads to the highest point of the cliff: exciting stuff.

La Robert-Marchal * 5 (E1 5b) 100ft

The long corner gives a steep sustained pitch with the crux right at the top, and a possible stance at half height. From the ledge above the corner, abseil off or climb the easy groove to the cliff top.

The right side of the cliff consists of a broad buttress, very steep in its upper section and with a massive fallen flake (so big that it is not instantly recognisable as such) stood in front of its centre. The top of the flake is the starting point for several climbs and can be reached by scrambling up behind the flake from the right.

At the top of the flake is a large cave, the first climb starts at the left edge of this and climbs the prominent deep groove to the left of the bulging head wall:

La Sophie *** 5+ (E1) 150ft

1. 70ft   4 (4c)   Climb the left edge of the cave then climb the wall to enter the left trending groove. Up this to a comfortable stance.

2. 80ft   5+ (5b)   The steep sustained groove gives a great pitch up an impressive line. Exit to the right to reach the cliff top.

L'Anne-Marie ** 5+ (E2) 160ft

1. 80ft   5- (5a)   From the right side of the cave climb the wall to an overhang and pull over this to gain and climb a broad rib to good ledges. A rather scruffy pitch that can be avoided by climbing the first pitch of La Sophie and moving right to a belay under the centre of the buttress.

2. 80ft   5+ (5b)   Climb the steep rounded arête directly above the stance until it is possible and very necessary to traverse left into the groove that splits the final nose. Bridge up this in ever more dramatic situations. A true "grand finale".

Two other very worthwhile pitches start from the stance on **L'Anne-Marie** and find their way through the sea of overhangs that lean over in such a menacing fashion.

Supreme Dimension ** 7b 80ft ◊

From the stance climb leftwards up the wall to the great bulge that caps it, "improvise" leftwards through this (it only overhangs 15ft) to a lowering point on the rim of the wall.

Le Lutin des Cimes ** 6b (E3 5c) 80ft

Start up the second pitch of **L'Anne-Marie** and continue directly up the hanging prow above past a deep hole which offers a semi-rest: brilliant climbing, outrageous positions.

The next buttress is the **ROCHER DE LA LIEDEKERKE,** a rather rambling crag consisting of a complex series of walls and towers that protrudes from the trees just to the west of the railway bridge. There are almost thirty routes on this face with only the best described here. At its tallest point the cliff is 180ft high though many of the routes do not go all the way to the top. For those that do the easiest descent is two abseils down the pillar to the left of the groove of **La Liedekerke** or alternatively take the easy descent down the deep gully to the right of the buttress.

The cliff is roughly divided into three sections by two major groove lines. Towards the left edge of the face is the long soaring groove of **La Liedekerke** whilst a way to the right is the conspicuous left facing twisting groove line that is followed by **Le Massacre de Saint-Valentin**. Between these two the cliff forms a broad arête with a pillar forming its crest. Almost all of the base of the cliff is undercut and so the starts of many of the routes are rather strenuous, though fortunately the holds are usually excellent. Take a big breath and steam on to clip the first bolt runner then relax and enjoy the rest of the route.

The pillar at the left side of the cliff has a couple of worthwhile combinations of routes. In both cases long pitches lead to a ledge at rather over half height, from where slightly harder extension pitches lead on to the cliff top. Alternatively the lower pitches can be done, followed by an abseil from the ledge system.

Symphonie d'Urinoir * 5- (HVS 5a) 100ft
Fifteen feet left of the huge diedre and just right of some recently developed and rather totty overhangs is a crack in a shallow corner. This is gained from directly below and followed to a stance on the left end of a long ledge system. Abseil from anchors at the far end of the ledge system or climb:

Le Sombrero * 5 (HVS 5a) 80ft ◊
A less sustained but worthwhile extension can be had by following the slanting crack rightwards towards the centre of the slab and then climbing direct to the top of the wall where belays and abseil anchors will be found. Alternatively walk off the back of the cliff (rightwards).

L'Emporte-Pièce * 4+ (VS 5a) 100ft
Begin roughly midway between the previous climb and the long groove system and climb bulging rock (crux) to gain access to the more amenable rock above. Graze off up the steep slab (or easy angled wall) to a good ledge with belays on the right. Either abseil from here or climb:

The steep lower section of Arête de Boisson, 4 (VS 4b), ROCHER DE L'ECRIN, MARCHE LES DAMES. Climber: Sherri Davy

Peku * 5 (HVS 5a) 80ft ◊

Step back left and climb the centre of the steep slab (or.....) trending slightly leftwards until the top of **Le Sombrero** is joined and followed to the cliff top.

La Liedekerke *** 4 (VS) 180ft

One of the great classics of Marche Les Dames, reasonably graded climbing up a stunning line. Start below a small cave at the base of the impressive groove line.

1. 100ft 3+ (4b)   Climb the steep wall (quickly) into the right side of the niche, have quick blow then move left and enter the soaring groove line. Climb this, generally straightforward to a ledge at the foot of the more imposing upper section.

2. 80ft 4 (4c)   Step right into the groove and follow it to the cliff top, superb.

High on the wall to the right of **La Liedekerke** is a diagonal line of overhangs formed by large hanging flake. A must for lovers of the sun tanned body, this is approached from the initial niche of **La Liedekerke**.

Les Bronzes ** 5+ (E2) 190ft

1. 40ft 3+ (4b)   Climb the steep wall into the niche, move left then belay in the base of the groove.

2. 150ft 5+ (5b)   Climb the wall to the right of the groove for 50ft to a narrow ledge then continue up more compact rock to reach the flake. Follow it leftwards to enter a shallow groove and climb this until it is possible to exit on the left.

The blunt arête of the buttress between the two prominent groove lines is climbed by

Calebar Étanche ** 5 (E1) 180ft

1. 120ft 5 (5b)   Start under an small groove below the central arête of the cliff. Climb this then continue in a direct line to a position below a bulge. Move left then pull back rightwards over this before climbing just left of the arête to a comfortable platform.

2. 60ft   Abseil off, or climb the slab to the cliff top.

La Moule * 5 (HVS 5a) 180ft

1. 120ft 5 (5a)   Start below the right edge of a hanging pillar 60ft up the face. Climb through the double overhang to reach the pillar and continue to its top. Follow a diagonal crack leftwards to the belay of the previous route.

2. 60ft   Abseil off, or climb the slab to the cliff top.

The impressive 25ieme Anniversaire Direct, 6a (E2 5b), MASSIF DU PARAPLUIE, BERDORF. Climber: Nigel Baker

Les Malaises * 6b (E3 6a) 130ft

Start just to the right of where the overhangs at the foot of the cliff fade out and climb the sustained pale wall to a possible yo-yo point at 25m. From here continue straight up the centre of the wall to a ledge and a belay. Either abseil from here or traverse right for 50ft along the ledge system to exit as for the next two routes.

To the right the base of the cliff juts forward and offers easy access to ledges at 50ft. There are two worthwhile routes that reach the ledges and then fine semi-independent ways to the cliff top.

La Carpette du Futur ** 5+ (E1) 210ft

1. 50ft   3 (Severe) Climb the corner on the left side of the straightforward rock to the comfortable "sit down type" ledge at 50ft.

2. 80ft   5+ (5b)   Climb the wall on the left to a discontinuous crack line that is followed as it curves over to the right. Continue in the same line to gain the top of the big groove of **Le Massacre de Saint-Valentin** and climb this to another spacious stance.

3. 80ft   4 (4b)   Trend left across the wall to enter a crack which is followed to the cliff top.

Le Massacre de Saint-Valentin *** 5 (HVS) 210ft

The other major classic of the cliff, a long and interesting climb that is never too hard.

1. 50ft   3 (Severe) Climb the centre of the projecting buttress to the spacious stance below the imposing curving groove.

2. 80ft   5 (5a)   Climb the groove which steepens up as height is gained. Fortunately the severely leaning upper section has adequate holds on the left wall so, although spectacular, the climbing is not too technical.

3. 80ft   4 (4c)   Trend left across the wall to enter a crack which is followed to the cliff top (as for the previous route).

To the right of the groove of **Le Massacre de Saint-Valentin** are a series of routes that start from the prominent large ledge at 50ft. They are generally not too hard, mostly being 4 (VS 4c'ish) and are all named after a series of strong beers, brewed here and over the border in Germany. The ledge can be reached by the groove on the left or a straightforward pitch leading to its centre. The routes climb the wall to reach another large ledge 90ft higher. From here either exit on the left by an easy groove or by the straightforward slab above the centre of the ledge.

To the right across a wooded gully is the last of the major buttresses in the **GROUPE DE BEEZ**. Above the railway bridge is the **Rocher de la Fanette** which is characterised by an impressive square-cut tower towards its left side, 100ft high, apparently smooth, and known as the Dalle de la Fanette. The first routes described are on this pillar which is reached by an awkward scramble from the right up a short buttress or more easily by a path that loops through the trees on the left.

The pillar is bounded on its left side by a chimney containing some giant jammed blocks. Starting just right of this awesome rift is

La Gamelle de Beethoven *** 6c (E4 6a) 100ft ◊

Start 3ft right of the big chimney and climb the wall passing the right edge of one bulge then climbing straight through two other bulges by sustained and technical climbing before continuing direct to the cliff top. Superb.

La Fanette *** 6b (E4 6a) 100ft ◊

Another great classic, considerably easier than its near neighbour though with the bolts further appart. Start in the centre of the wall and climb straight up pockety rock to a hole then continue up a couple of discontinous cracks (runout) to resting ledges below the black bulges. It is possible to belay here but that rather breaks the spell. When you are ready for it step left and pull through the bulges with difficulty (and perhaps a bit of a slap) then continue more easily to the top of the buttress.

Plus Beau Que Moi Tu Meurs ** 6b+ (E4 6a) 70/100ft ◊

The poor relation of the trio but still worth doing. Start just left of the chimney crack to the right of the white pillar under a diagonal overlap. Climb to and through the overlap then continue up the right edge of the wall just left of the arête until things ease and ledges are reached. Either lower off from these or climb the short leaning wall above the ledges to the cliff top.

Les Bonbons *** 4- (VS) 130ft

The steep chimney that bounds the right side of the white pillar of the Dalle de Fanette gives a classic way up the cliff, especially recommended for those who have a sweet tooth. Approach from the foot of the cliff via an awkward projecting flake.

1. 70ft   4- (4b)   Climb the steep lower section of the chimney using a variety of traditional techniques (I bet you thought you would never need them) until a stance on the right can be reached.

2. 30ft   3+ (Severe) Step back left and make a couple of tricky moves up the steep corner to reach easier angled rock. Amble leftwards up this to a stance under the final obstacle.

3. 30ft   4- (4b)   Climb into the corner and bridge up it steeply to a sudden arrival on the cliff top in the vicinity of a substantial and convenient tree belay.

Tribotechnique ** 6a (E2 5c) 80ft ◊

The smart wall to the right of the chimney of **Les Bonbons** gives a good steep pitch on fine rock. Step right onto the wall and climb it to a bulge at 50ft. Pull leftwards through this and continue with less difficulty to ledges and a lower off.

The next prominent feature down the slope to the right of the chimney of **Les Bonbons** is a steep juggy crack line. This is the first pitch of

L'Ivrogne * 4+ (VS) 170ft**

1. 80ft   4+ (4c)   Climb the steep crack to ledges then step right to follow the obvious continuation to a stance at the top of a series of stepped ledges.

2. 40ft   4 (4b)   Follow the twisting crack to the right of the arête to reach easier ground then move left to a stance below the head wall.

3. 50ft   3+ (Severe) Head up right to the crest of the buttress then climb a short wall that gives access to the groove leading to the cliff top and the end of an intoxicating trip.

Innominate ** 5+ (E2 5b) 100ft ◊

Start just down the slope from the crack of **L'Ivrongne** below a line of spaced green bolts (red belay bolt) and above a bit of a drop. Climb steeply rightwards through the initial bulges on "funny" rock then climb the wall trending slightly leftwards to reach the ledge at the top of the initial crack on the previous climb. Step left and head up the ever steepening wall to a final few tricky moves up the terminal pillar. Good sport.

The next six routes start around the toe of the buttress where there are a series of closely-packed, colour-coded pitches. It is usual to lower from the spacious ledge above the steep lower wall though there are colour coded extensions to some of the routes up the wall above the ledges.

Diabolique Cougnet * 5 (E1 5b) 80ft ◊**

The left-most bolt ladder (blue) tackles the left side of the arête, starting just right of a projecting flake. It starts on a pedestal and gives a pleasant pitch on good holds, with the run-out section being easier than it looks (sighs of relief). Climb rightwards up the initial leaning wall to a niche then keep left of the arête all the way to the lower offs.

Le Pilier de Barnotin * 5 (E1 5b) 80ft ◊

The crest of the arête is followed direct via a cave at 15ft. The lower section is hard work but it eases as height is gained. Good positions though rather escapable in its upper reaches.

The steep initial
section of
Diabolique
Cougnet,
5 (E1 5b),
ROCHER DE LA
FANETTE,
MARCHE LES
DAMES.
Climbers:
Nigel Baker and
Andy Watts

Sister Jane **
5+ (E1 5c) 100ft
◊
The line of red
bolts is followed
to the roof where
awkward stren-
uous moves lead
to ledges; it's all a
matter of finding
the good holds.
Continue directly
up the wall to the
large ledges. A
short extension
pitch is available
up the smooth
wall above, or
lower off.

Frère Jacques * **5+ (E2 5b) 80ft** ◊
The steep initial wall leads to resting ledges (rather spaced yellow bolts); then
continue to the ledges above, join the blue bolt ladder after the 4th clip. Lower off
or climb the short smooth extension above.

La Loup Phique * **5+ (E1 5b) 80ft** ◊
The right-hand line on this section of rock has a steep, butch start and again eases
as height is gained. From the ledges lower off or climb the short steep wall above
the right side of the ledges (sounds familiar doesn't it).

To the right of the toe of the buttress there is a deep corner with a wide crack in its back. This is the start of

Le Piment Royal *** 4+ (VS) 190ft

A classic route up the full height of the cliff, direct and interesting with good stances so that the whole route can be enjoyed to the full.

1. 80ft   4 (4b)   Climb the corner groove to its top and then tackle the short wall to reach a good ledge.

2. 60ft   4+ (4c)   Step left and follow the long twisting crack line with sustained moves to a stance on a ledge by a big block.

3. 50ft   3+ (Severe) Climb the short wall to gain entry to the easy chimney groove that runs to the cliff top.

To the right and a short scramble up the slope is the final section of the **ROCHER DE LA FANETTE**, known as the **SECTEUR SOLIDARNOSC** and consisting of a vertical lower wall leading to a large ledge at about 30 feet, and above which is a higher and steeper wall. There are a selection of pleasant routes here on good rock, in a slightly out of the way situation, a good spot to get away from it all. There are enough routes for a pleasant couple of hours' sport here.

At the left edge of the lower wall is a deep chimney that gives easy access (though not that easy in training shoes) to the ledge that cuts across the face. Three feet right of this is a short line of red bolts that marks the lower section of;

La Digitale Pourpre * 5- (HVS) 105ft

1. 25ft   4 (4c)   Climb the short steep wall to a belay at the foot of the ramp that rises from the left end of the ledge system.

2. 80ft   5- (5a)   Climb the ramp until it runs out under a small overhang. From here traverse left for 6ft then climb back rightwards up the steep wall to the cliff top (escaping off to the left below this final steeping is definitely taboo).

La Paty Noire ** 5+ E1 100ft ◊

1. 25ft   4 (4b)   15ft right of the chimney is a short hanging crack protected by blue bolts. Reach this and follow it to the ledge and a belay to the right under a steep sentry box.

2. 75ft   5+ (5b)   Climb the right edge of the sentry box and continue up mighty steep rock on generous holds until the angle begins to ease. Press on (strength permitting) to a lower off just below the highest point of the wall.

To the right of the start of the last route is a tall flake at the foot of the cliff and just to the right of this is a left trending break. Starting at the foot of this is

Le Mouron Rouge *** 5+ (E2) 100ft ◊

1. 25ft   5 (5a)   Climb straight up the wall (blue bolts) and through a hanging flake to a stance and belays on the large ledge.

2. 75ft 5+ (5b) Climb slightly leftwards up the leaning wall on superb though occasionally spaced pockets until the angle drops back a little. A couple of more technical moves are needed to climb a tiny pillar, first right then left, above which more good holds lead rapidly to the lower offs. A cracker.

The steep corner which bounds the right side of the upper face is approached up the lower wall by

La Voie du Lamier Jaune ** 5+ (E1) 90ft

1. 40ft 5 (5a) Start at a flake crack to the right of the blue bolts of the previous climb and follow this until it is possible to step right amd climb rightwards to a stance on the upper section of the large ledge.

2. 50ft 5+ (5b) Step left and follow the steep imposing groove, generally on good holds, with awkward moves to get established on a jammed block. Exit to the right.

To the right the final section of the lower wall is steep and smooth looking. There are several worthwhile quick ticks here, technical and well protected, just the job.

Gymcobiloba * 6a+ (E2 6a) 40ft ◊

The left-hand line, just to the right of the flake crack. Climb first left then right and finally back left to reach the lower offs.

Le Jardin Mogol * 6a (E2 5c) 40ft ◊

Just to the right again, sustained and fingery climbing up steep rock.

The final two pitch climb on this section of cliff is

La Voie du Listeron ** 5+ (E2) 80ft

1. 40ft 5+ (5b) Climb the precarious shallow dièdre in the centre of the lower wall to a belay on the right side of the large ledge.

2. 40ft 5+ (5b) Climb another groove and then the leaning wall above until it is possible to pull onto the right arête. Finish easily.

Two short tough pitches complete the selection here:

Pétales Hurlants * 6b (E3 6a) 40ft ◊

The technical and sustained wall just right of the open groove proves to be the hardest pitch on the lower wall.

Glasnost * 6b (E3 6a) 40ft ◊

The vague crack line immediately left of the arête is followed to a tricky finish.

To the right of the **ROCHER DE LA FANETTE** is a steep gully (care required if used as a descent) and across this are the two final buttresses in the **GROUPE**

DE BEEZ. The first of these is the **AIGUILLES DU NOBLE** which has about ten routes mostly grade **4 (c.VS)** and about 70ft high, including some fine-looking, bolt-protected crack lines. Further right is the **ROCHER CARIBOU** which is 50 feet high and has some fifteen routes, the best of which again follow fine crack lines with the occasional smooth faces. These are mostly **6a (E2)** though there are routes up to 7a in grade. This cliff has been closed seasonally up to 15th July because it is home to nesting peregrines. Please respect these arrangments.

Classical pocket pulling on Une Sale Histoire de Reglettes et des Trous 6a (E2 5c) on the (at present) closed ROCHER DU CHARBONNIER, MARCHE LES DAMES. Climber: Nigel Baker

MOZET

INTRODUCTION
A pleasant array of south facing buttresses and pinnacles located in quiet birch woodland. On the left side of the cliff the trees rather encroach though the right side is more open to the sun and as a consequence is more popular. The rocks are not very high (up to about 80 feet) and they have quite an English air about them. In fact if it was not for the copious fixed protection and the fact that the cliff gets so much sunshine the place could have been lifted straight from the wooded banks of Dovedale.

The rock is generally good though loose patches do occur and a few of the routes are exceptionally polished. There is not a lot here to tempt the hot shot but there are an acceptable number of routes in the middle and lower grades. The cliffs were developed by Flemish speaking Belgians, hence the names of some of the routes are rather a mouthful. Although Mozet lacks the grandeur of Freyr it is worth a visit for a bit of peace and quiet, a pleasant day's sport being guaranteed.

GEOGRAPHY
The cliff consists of four discrete rock masses. On the extreme left and directly behind the cafe of "La Refuge" is the long and rather dusty wall of the **ARENDMASSIEF**. This section of cliff tends to suffer from soil being washed down from the bank above, though the routes described are generally clean. Across the gully to the right is the conspicuous narrow pinnacle of the **EEKHOORNMASSIEF** which has a prominent wire cable encircling its summit. This offers the prospect of safe and easy retreat from the summit and is a suitable target to jump for if you find yourself in total extremist on the final moves of your chosen objective.

Another gully to the right (or technically another branch of the same gully) separates the pinnacle from the broader mass of rock of the **GEMSMASSIEF**. From the summit of this it is usual to either abseil/lower back down your line of ascent or reverse **Cyclamen (V.Diff)** on the short west face of the tower. The final feature is the face of the **STEENBOKMASSIEF** with a prominent slender pinnacle standing in front of its centre and a curious cave/arch cutting through its right side. There are descents to both left and right and it is also possible to scramble down through the arch.

APPROACHES
The cliff is located above the small village of Samson which is situated in a narrow valley that runs south from the main valley of the Meuse to the east of Namur. From Namur follow the N90 eastwards along the south bank of the river for 12 kilometres. A right turn leads round a series of bends into the village. On the left

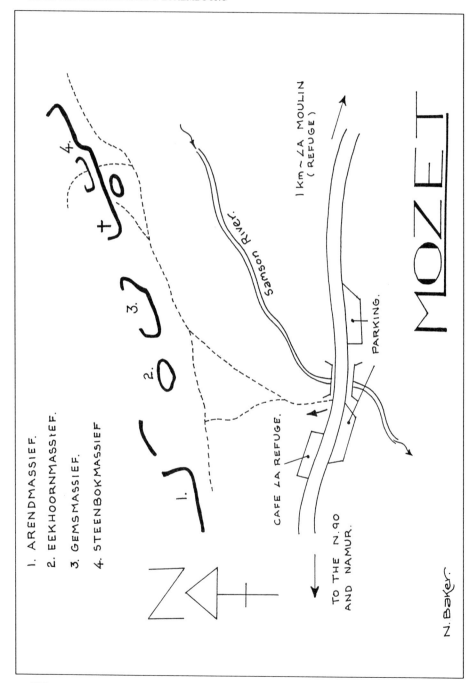

1. ARENDMASSIEF.
2. EEKHOORNMASSIEF.
3. GEMSMASSIEF.
4. STEENBOKMASSIEF

Samson River.

1 km ~ LA MOULIN (REFUGE)

MOZET

PARKING.

CAFE LA REFUGE.

TO THE N.90 AND NAMUR.

N. Baker.

is the cafe "La Refuge" (if you like ice-cream try one of their "Dame Blanches") and opposite here is limited parking to either side of the bridge over the Samson river. Immediately to the right of the cafe a narrow track leads alongside the river and up the bank to the cliff two minutes away.

> **Note:** The out-of-print guide book to the cliff uses UIAA grades. In an attempt to avoid too much confusion I have converted these to (approximate?) French grades in keeping with the rest of this book. I accept responsibility for any anomalies.

The routes are described from left to right.

THE ARENDMASSIEF

The long wall directly behind the cafe has a large number (over forty) of mostly hard routes that are often rather dirty. Clustered around the right arête of the cliff are some easier routes that tend to be cleaner. Some climbs have lower offs; others top out on to the steep bank above where substantial trees offer suitable abseil anchors.

Towards the left side of the cliff is an obvious cave with a flat rock floor reached by a short scramble. Pulling out of the left side of this is

Slak ** 6c (E4 6a) 80ft ◊

Marked by a line of new bolts. Pull up the leaning wall (surprising holds) then swing left to reach and follow the sustained wall direct to the cliff top following the steep groove left of the prow in its upper section.

To the right is a prominent large deep corner in the upper half of the cliff. This is

Sneeuwhaas * 5 (HVS 5a) 80ft ◊

The base of the corner is reached by a diagonal ascent from the right crossing slabby rock. Follow the corner steeply and at its closure traverse across the right wall to reach the cliff top. The obvious direct finish is called **Smurf** and this is a grade harder than the regular finish.

To the right of the deep corner is an open brown groove that is often a touch scruffy, climbed by the original route of the cliff

Arend * 5+ (E1 5b) 80ft ◊

Start below and right of the groove and climb up and across a slab to reach its base. Up the groove to the cliff top. A route that could do with a good wash and brush up.

Pirana ** 6b (E3 6a) 80ft ◊

Start just to the right of the previous route and follow the line of bolts diagonally to the right then straight up the wall by sustained and interesting climbing.

To the right is a slab running up towards a curious water worn channel (30 feet from the right edge of the wall). This provides the line of one of the better routes on the cliff though it is not quite as exciting as the name might suggest.

Adrenaline *** 6a (E2 5c) 80ft ◊

Climb the slab to steeper rock (old slings) then follow the interesting scoopy groove to a pull over a bulge and a finish directly up the wall.

Right again is an arête that forms the right edge of the **ARENDMASSIEF** where the cliff swings round to form the east-facing side wall of a gully. To the left of the arête is a left-facing corner groove that leads up to a good ledge half way up the face.

Vlinder * 6a (E2 5c) 80ft ◊

Follow the left-facing corner with prominent bolts in its left wall to the ledge (possible stance) then step right and climb a scoop to a tricky overhang above which easier climbing leads to the cliff top.

Geit * 5 (VS 4c) 70ft ◊

Start just around to the right of the arête at a prominent left-slanting crack. Climb the crack to the ledge of the previous route (possible stance over on the left) then continue up the groove to its end and step out to a pleasant finish up the face on the right.

Koala ** 6c (E4 6b) 60ft ◊

To the right of the slanting crack of **Geit** is a smooth but well-equipped face. Climb this as direct as possible. The start is tough and so is the rest of it, a little less of a cuddly plaything than its namesake!

Vos * 5 (HVS 5a) 60ft ◊

The final feature of any note on this face is this continuous crack line that gives a pleasant pitch.

To the right and on the rear face of the tower are another dozen or so short routes. They are mostly grade 3 and 4 (V.Diff to Severe), with just a couple of harder offerings. They are generally a bit too short to merit description.

Across the gully to the right is the prominent slender tower of the **EEKHOORNMASSIEF**. This is basically triangular in section and has three facets (obvious really), the south, north-east and west faces. The routes are described in anti-clockwise direction starting with the left edge of the south face as this is the usual point of arrival. The customary descent is by threading and lowering from the substantial wire cable that encircles the summit.

Poema * 6a+ (E3 6a) 60ft ◊

Quite a tough little number, with just a touch of loose rock. From the bottom corner of the wall climb a short hanging groove and a tricky bulge. At two-thirds height swing left to pass a particularly blank bit of rock, before steeping back right to finish.

The line up the smooth right side of the face is called **Fret** though it doesn't appear to have been free climbed: any takers? Around to the right in the centre of the north east face is the start of

Schorpion * 6b (E3 6a) 50ft ◊

Follow the groove with sustained interest (ie. difficulty) until it becomes possible to pull out leftwards onto the south side of the tower. You might expect a sting in the tail but in fact easier climbing remains.

Eikel * 4 (Severe 4a) 20ft ◊

The short side of the tower is climbed starting from a shoulder and passing a couple of peg runners.

Eikel Variation * 4 (Severe 4a) 40ft

Start a short distance down the bank to the right of the regular route and climb the wall until it is possible to step left onto the shoulder to join and finish as for the Voie Normal.

Across the gully to the right is the more extensive and more open **GEMSMASSIEF,** basically another detached tower. Higher up the gully between these two rock masses is the short wall of the **SCHOOLBANK** which as the name suggests offers a suitable place for basic instruction. There are half a dozen lines of grade **2** and **3** (**Diff** and **V.Diff**), and as might be expected they are rather polished.

Across the gully the **GEMSMASSIEF** has some worthwhile climbs though once again some of them are very well burnished. The left side of the face is steep and not very accommodating and although two of the routes have apparently been free climbed, the archaic bolts and cobwebs on the rock suggest that they are far from popular. Immediately left of the arête at the point where the footpath arrives is **Roodborstje 7a?** and towards the left side of the face is **Baviaan 6c?**. With a bit of a clean-up they would offer good technical climbs. Just to the right is the rather more popular

Korhoen + Direct Finish ** 6a (E2 5b) 50ft ◊

Climb rightwards up a flake and over small overhang to enter a groove. Either follow this to the easy ridge above or, better, pull leftwards out of this onto the face as soon as possible and finish directly up this.

The roof to the right is climbed by stepping in from the right by the rather trivial **Gibbon 5 (HVS 5a)** ◊. Once past the roof trend left up easier rock.

Immediately to the right of the roof is a flaky groove leading to a grey slab.

Alpenkauw 4+ (HVS 5b) 40ft P ◊

An interesting insight as to just how polished limestone can get. Climb the groove to the foot of the slab then skate up it to the top using good but spaced and frictionless finger holds. Sneaking off right is taboo at the grade.

To the right the cliff is split by a deep corner. Set in the left wall of this is a groove:

Linde 3 (V.Diff) 30ft P ◊

Follow the groove throughout.

Berk 2 (Diff) 30ft P ◊

The deep corner gives a pleasant but polished scramble.

To the right of the corner is a large prominent hanging block fifteen feet up the cliff. Passing round the left side of this is

Kaketoe * 6a (E2 5c) 50ft P ◊

An interesting climb though with a rather unsatisfactory lower section. Climb to the block then step left before making tricky moves up and back right to gain a polished ledge with difficulty. (A direct version is reachy E3 6a.) Continue up and right to the cliff top by pleasantly sustained moves.

Uil ** 5 (HVS 5a) 50ft P ◊

This rather more fulfilling route gains the groove on the right side of the hanging block then continues direct to join the last couple of moves of the previous climb.

To the right is a smooth open corner:

Gems * 6a (E1 6a) 50ft P ◊

The groove gives a pleasant though slippery pitch with a short sharp and very safe crux section, a technical jewel. At the top of the groove move right to finish on the fittingly situated arête.

In the nose of the buttress to the right is an impossible-looking hanging corner and just around the arête is a thin leaning crack containing a wealth of well hammered ironmongery:

Vink * 6b (E2 6a) 40ft ◊

Layback through the initial bulge with difficulty on rock that is more solid than it looks then follow the crack until forced out to the right just below the top of the tower. Finish easily.

Cyclamen 3+ (V.Diff) 30ft ◊

The short side of the tower is the usual descent, though it is also the easiest way to bag the summit.

Across the next gully is the most popular section of the cliff, the **STEENBOKMASSIEF**. There are over forty routes here including some of the best offerings at **Mozet**. On the highest point of the cliff is a substantial iron cross (now that's what I call a solid belay) and the outlook from here is quite sublime. On the left side of this section of cliff is a short wall containing several grooves and capped by a large tree on its top right corner. There are several low grade routes here suitable for instructional purposes or for the very timid. All of them are rather polished so here is an opportunity to appraise your foot work; lose five points for every time you skate off a hold.

Nigritell 3 V.Diff 20ft P

The short groove at the left side of the wall starting over a small bulge.

Pier 5 (VS 5a) 20ft P

The centre of the short buttress just to the right is climbed until it is possible to step left and follow a short crack to the top.

Netel 3 (V.Diff) 20ft P

The deep groove just to the right.

Enzian 3 (V.Diff) 30ft P

Climb the pillar to the right of the corner of **Netel** by following a flake crack out to the right to a finish in a pleasing situation.

Grizzly 5+ (HVS 5b) 30ft ◊

The arête just to the right gives a technical little offering.

Mier 4 (Severe) 30ft ◊

The smooth corner just right of the arête is followed to a tricky finish.

Boterbloem 3 (V.Diff) 20ft ◊

The easy corner on the right side of the wall leads to a belay by the tree.

Across an easy break is another **SCHOOLBANK** with a selection of very mild routes with substantial belays at the top. This is delineated on its right side by a large flake climbed by the start of

Soldanella * 4 (VS 4b) 50ft P ◊

Climb the flaky corner to the top of the pedestal then trend right up the pleasant face above.

143

**The thin central section of Panda 6b (E1 6a), STEENBOKMASSIEF, MOZET.
Climber: Colin Binks**

Panda * **6b (E1 6a) 50ft P** ◊
The thin crack in the centre of the wall gives a technical but very safe little problem

144

easing rapidly above the crux moves. A good choice if you wonder whether you can climb 6a.

Condor * 4 (VS 4c) 50ft ◊

The shallow groove just to the left of the pinnacle is entered steeply, then smoke up it to where it fizzles out, continue direct.

To the right is the prominent slender pinnacle standing a short distance away from the main face. There are five routes that climb this and then stride across on to the cliff before continuing up polished rock to the top of the buttress arriving right by the summit cross.

Vis * 5 (HVS 5a) 50ft ◊

Climb the chimney between the tower and the main edge near its western end bridging back to the tower as and when needed. Eventually it is necessary to abandon the pinnacle (don't push off it too hard, it may fall over) and climb the easy but polished arête to the top of the crag.

Luis * 6a (E1 5c) 50ft ◊

Follow the west arête of the tower to its tip by way of a couple of tricky moves then stride boldly across (or gibber hopelessly) before continuing without further ado as for the previous route.

Marmot 5+ (E2 5c) 50ft ◊

The south face of the tower is tackled via a tricky bulge and a couple of bolder moves to reach the right arête. Plod on to the tip and then continue as for the previous routes.

Vlooi * 5 (HVS 5a) 50ft ◊

The east arête of the pinnacle is steep but has big enough holds to make it a pleasant outing. Finish as for the previous route.

Steenbok ** 4 (VS 4b) 50ft P ◊

The easiest way up this section of the cliff. Climb the inside wall of the pinnacle close to its eastern arête (the tall can bridge back to the main cliff in places). Do a headstand on the summit then step across to the main edge and gambol up the wall to the cross.

To the right is the odd cave/tunnel/arch that cuts through the cliff. There used to be a host of aid routes around, across and through this oddity, and I am not sure how many of them have gone free. If you fancy involving yourself with this feature the best bet is Belgium's answer to **Spider's Web**.

Zwarte Weduwe ** 6a (E2 5c) 40ft

A route that is hard to lead, harder to second and almost impossible to describe! Start in the back right corner of the arch (looking in) and chimney up into the roof. Shuffle forward (slings) and make difficult moves to get across into the groove in the hanging wall in the roof of the arch. Up this then either exit left, right or sneak through the tunnel and escape via the "back passage". All very strange.

To the right of the tunnel entrance is a broad high wall containing some of the best routes on the cliff. The first two start under the right edge of the arch.

Zwaluw ** 7a 70ft ◊

Start on the arête and climb steeply to reach the base of the prominent smooth "slab" that bristles with eight bolts. Improvise your way up this eventually moving right to join the final few moves of the next climb.

Rups ** 5 (HVS 5a) 70ft ◊

Start at the name **Lintworm** [a left to right girdle of this wall at 4 (VS 4c)] painted on the rock and move out right to gain the long groove line. This is followed past a big red sling with sustained interest all the way to the cliff top.

Gier ** 6b (E3 6a) 70ft ◊

A sustained climb well "giered" after the rather bold start. Around to the right of the cave is a block on the ground, start below overhangs about ten feet left of this. Slant up to the right on good but spaced holds to gain entry to a steep groove and climb it to a tricky leftward exit. Continue up the fine sustained groove above.

To the right the lower section of the cliff is steep and the upper part is a fine grey slab of excellent rock. The two old aid routes up this have been rebolted and now look both hard and excellent. The left-hand line is **Lynx** and the right-hand line is **Piguin**. Unfortunately I have not been able to come up with any grades for the routes though they appear on abseil to be at least 6c (E4); you will just have to go exploring.

Just right again is a continuous groove rising from a cave at ground level. The groove is

Slang ** 4 (VS 4b) 70ft P ◊

Enter the groove steeply and follow it as it deepens, with continuous interest. One of the original classics of the cliff, hence its high quality lustre.

To the right is an open slabby groove with a narrow flat overhang 15ft up it, before the cliff swings round to face east.

Beest * 5+ (E1 5b) 70ft ◊

Not as grand as its namesake on Beeston Tor but still worthwhile. Climb the shallow open groove to the left side of the overhang then continue up the steep

wall to gain entry to the deeper hanging groove above. Climb this to a ledge then either finish easily or, better, step out onto the exposed arête on the right and finish up this.

Salamander ** 5 (HVS 5a) 70ft ◊

Climb to the right side of the flat roof and pull over into the rightward-slanting groove. Climb this awkwardly to the arête and finish more easily.

Specht * 7a (E4 6b) 70ft ◊

The smooth-looking bolted wall to the left of the arête is at least as hard as it looks, and it looks totally impossible. Steel fingers and technical wizardry required.

Hagedis * 5 (HVS 6a) 60ft P ◊

Just right of the arête is a tall perched flake. Climb over this and past a second flake to gain a sloping ledge with great difficulty (try jumping). Step left and follow the easier arête to the top.

Boa ** 6c+ (E3 6b) 40ft

The thin slanting crack in the face up the slope to the right (the one with the big new bolts) is technically titillating, with a couple of very thin moves at two-thirds height.

Adder 4 (VS 4b) 30ft

The rather gloomy corner on the right has a steep start and good holds above, the last offering of any significance on the cliff.

Nearing the top of the fine open groove of Salamander, 5 (HVS 5a), STEENBOKMASSIEF, MOZET. Climber: Dave Spencer

OTHER AREAS

Driving up and down the deeply incised valleys of the Meuse and its tributaries, the considerable amount of steep exposed and underdeveloped limestone is quite a surprise to climbers from north of the English Channel. There is also another set of cliffs that protrude from the side of the Ourthe valley to the south of Liège. In both these areas several of the cliffs have been developed and others have been largely ignored. Generally these are not worth an extended visit at present, though if you want to get away from it all or to do a bit of exploring then a couple of these areas may be worth considering for a visit. In the following notes **(?)** means the crag is of questionable worth, **(*)** means it may be worth a visit if you are in the area, **(**)** means definitely worth looking in on if you are passing, and **(***)** means possibly worth a trip from afar. On this scale **FREYR** would get **(*****)** and **DAVE** **(****)**. These notes do not aim to be exhaustive but give pointers to some of the more prominent bits of rock scattered around the countryside

The cliffs are described from north to south down the Meuse Valley starting from Namur, followed by the tributaries of the Meuse and finally back up the Ourthe Valley from south to north, effectively forming an anti-clockwise tour of these other areas.

THE MEUSE VALLEY
Carrière de Tailfer (*)
Three kilometres to the south of Dave on the same side of the river is a huge quarried slab, with a great square chunk sawn out of its lower left side. A three pitch route **La Grand Dalle (***) 250ft VS 4a,4a,4a,** climbs the slab at its highest point and gives a most unusual outing being sustained, fully bolt-protected and with never a vestige of a decent hold. Access to the slab used to be unrestricted though I noticed on my last visit that the quarry was being used to store road stone. Check the situation locally.

The "underside" of the slab is a very steep north-facing wall of natural limestone running steeply up the hillside. There appears to be the potential for some sport the wrong side of vertical here.

The Rochers des Fresnes (*)
An impressive streaked wall that overhangs the road and railway line between Lustin and Tailer. Development of the main section would cause obvious problems though there have been some developments away to the right. Bags of scope.

The Rochers du Paradou (**)
Further south from the last crag and on the same side of the river, between Godinne and Yvoir, is this steep 150ft high slab with a prominent white scar on

Following the second pitch of Le Grand Dalle, 4 (VS 4b) CARRIERE DE TAILFER.
Climber: Sherri Davy

its right side. There are about ten routes on here from **4 (VS 4b)** on the left to **6b**
(E3 6a) on the right where the rock becomes much more compact. Unfortunately
access to the cliff has been closed for a couple of years because of its proximity
to the railway line. Watch the notice board at the Cafe Chamonix for any change
in the situation.

Rochers de Champalle (*?)**
The superb and impressive walls set back on the east bank of the river to the south
of Yvoir are closed to climbing for ecological reasons.

Le Sex Shop (*)
A series of small quarried walls with a dozen or so "plonk on" face routes 6b to
7b. If you don't expect too much you won't be too disappointed. The cliff is visible

in the trees just south of the impressive pillar holding up the motorway bridge to the south of Dinant and is reached from a minor road running parallel to the main road.

Rochers de Waulsort (*)

To the south of Freyr and on the same side of the river there are extensive cliffs opposite the small village of Waulsort.

The cliffs take the form of a buttress with double overhangs at the northern end, a pleasant small domed buttress in field in the centre and a series of impressive fins protruding from the hillside towards the southern end. There are only a few routes here (mainly easy ones on the domed buttress) but there is a lot of potential. The cliffs can be approached by walking upstream from this base of the cliffs at Freyr though the easiest access is to catch the foot ferry across the river at Waulsort. The ferry is free but if you don't tip the ferry man you may have to swim back!! If you decide not to climb there is a very pleasant bar at the drop-off point from the ferry.

THE LESSE VALLEY

The River Lesse is best known for its canoe descents. It is possible to leave your car at the lowest point of the river, just short of where it joint the Meuse, and catch a train to its upper reaches. From here you can canoe back down the valley stopping off at as many "buvettes" as you need (canoeing can be such thirsty work).

There is a lot of rock exposed in the Lesse valley and very little of it has been developed.

Rocher des Copères (*)

Around the campsite at Villatoile (see Introduction) there are a series of pinnacles and towers that protrude from the valley side. There are quite a few bolted low-grade routes on these that may be worth visiting if you are camping in the area and normally operate in the lower grades.

Rochers du Castel (?)

A short distance up the Lesse valley from Villatoile is an immensely impressive and still inhabited castle sat on top of a hardly less impressive cliff. The fact that the castle walls rise straight from the top of the cliff may cause problems (as may the boiling oil), though there is supposed to have been some development. There are also two fine pieces of rock on the other side of the valley, unfortunately they rise straight out of the river.

Aiguilles de Châleux (** for looking at, * for climbing on)

A very impressive set of towers that soar 200 feet straight from the waters of the Lesse. Use of binoculars points to there having been some development here in the past as there are relics of aid gear in many places. There are a few recent bolt ladders in impressive situations. To the left of the main cliff is a massive cave entrance (projects galore) and up the hills to the right is a smooth bolted slab (no grade known) and a slender leaning pinnacle, the **Aiguilles de Châleux**, with a 50ft *** 3 (Severe)** up its short side.

The easiest approach to the base of the cliff (and the ubiquitous "buvette") is by turning west (looping under the road) up the Lesse valley from the bridge over the river on the road between Hulsonniaux and Veves and following this minor road for a couple of kilometres. This approach passes right under the foot of the **Rochers des Éperviers (*)** an impressive buttress in the trees on the left of the road that has a couple of routes and some scope. From the parking by the cafe cross the river using the railway bridge just downstream.

Another approach for the top of the cliffs is to park at the nature reserve to the south of Furfooz and follow a good path westwards for half a kilometre. The cliffs will appear on the left in the trees.

The Rocher de Anticlinal (?)
The obvious arched outcrop above the N86 just west of Han sur Less has been climbed on in the past. I am not sure why.

THE OURTHE VALLEY
There are quite a number of outcrops scattered along the banks of the Ourthe valley that runs south from the city of Liège, though many of them are of little significance. Those listed here are the more notable and they are listed from south to north.

The Rocher de Hotton (*/**)
Cross the river northwards in the centre of Hotton and turn immediately right towards Erezee. At a sharp left bend 350 metres along here is parking in a small loop road by the bar called the "Commanderie". To the left of this a narrow muddy track leads to the cliff in 150 metres.

There are approximately 100 routes here on some impressive sheets of rock, up to 140ft high and from 3 to 7a. Unfortunately many of the climbs are polished almost beyond belief. The central section of the cliff is the most impressive and consists of a steep slab with some thin crack and hard face routes. Further to the right is a large low-angled slab with some well bolted 3s and 4s, possibly the highlight of the cliff. If you climb at these grades the place may be worth a visit.

Roche du Calvaire (***)
A short cliff of considerable impact. The cliff contains twenty or so very well-bolted routes from 6b to 8a though mostly in the 7s. The crag is not extensive but it is very steep and pocketed. For climbers operating in the upper echelons there are a couple of good days' sport here.

The crag is located on the west bank of the Ourthe on the outskirts of the small town of Bomal, 14 kilometres north of Hotton. Cross the bridge over the river and turn immediately to the right and drive alongside the railway line to a new breeze-block building at the end of the track. The cliff is visible two minutes away.

Roche aux Corneilles (?)

An impressive piece of rock, 140 feet high, that shows little sign of modern development though it has obviously been used extensively for aid practice in the past. The crag rises from the river 2 kilometres north of Bomal (see above). A short distance north of the cliff is parking in a short loop of road on a bend (care required). Walk back down the road and descend the STEEP bank to the foot of the cliff. The best-looking line is the long groove to the right of the central mass of the crag in two pitches. The steep walls to the right of this show some promise and the left side of the cliff looks superb but a tough proposition with a lot of very steep, high quality rock.

Rocher de Sy (***)

An extensive area of cliffs around the idyllic village of the same name, about 20 kilometres north of Hotton and 4 kilometres south of Hamoir. There are nine buttresses upstream from the village and another six downstream, with routes up to 150 feet high. Many of the cliffs tend to be slabby and there are a large number of low grade routes here. The polished nature of the rock is a problem, but perhaps no more than back home. The cliffs have been leased by members of the Dutch Alpine Club (a contradiction in terms?) and their equipping of the routes is not up to the standard of the Belgian Alpine Club so carry a rack. There has been some friction in the past between Dutch and Belgian climbers, both here and at Freyr. You are apparently supposed to get a licence to climb on the cliffs from Liège, though we found we were not bothered by the other climbers.

The place is probably best suited to climbers operating in the V.Diff to V.S. grades who want to get away from the crowds, and to climb in lovely surroundings. There are campsites in the area.

LUXEMBOURG

ROCHERS DU WANTERBAACH - BERDORF

INTRODUCTION:

A large part of the diminutive principality of Luxembourg consists of high rolling farm land dissected by the tributaries of the River Moselle. The steep sided valleys are too precipitous for agriculture and so have kept their heavy forest cover. High quality sandstone outcrops in many of these valleys are usually in the form of isolated towers and buttresses. To climbers who have visited the delightful but diminutive outcrop of Kyloe in the Wood in darkest Northumberland, the cliffs at Berdorf will have a familiar feel albeit on a much grander scale. For the newcomer the place really is somewhere rather special: colourful walls and towers of superb rock with plentiful fixed protection and set in a haunting forest of giant trees. There are jamming cracks here to delight any jaded gritstoner and face climbs of the highest calibre. For many years the use of chalk on these cliffs was frowned on though now it appears to be acceptable to have a dip as and when required. The tame nuthatches that pick around the base of the cliff add a little magical touch and the view from the cliff tops is sylvan. Please treat the place with the respect it deserves, keep to the paths as the sandy soil is easily eroded, don't litter and please be respectful to the locals.

The undercut and ever-dry nature of the base of much of the cliff along with sandy bottoms (nothing worse) offers the potential for superb bouldering at Berdorf itself and in many of the outlying valleys. Whether you like your bouldering to be fiercely technical (crimping and cranking) or strenuously draining (pumping and slapping) there is plenty here to keep you happy; go off and search out your ideal problems, they are waiting for you out there somewhere.

HOW TO GET THERE

The cliffs are situated close to the charming small village of Berdorf about 25 kilometres to the north-east of the major city of Luxembourg. From the Belgium/ Luxembourg border (petrol is cheaper on the Luxembourg side of the frontier) follow the toll-free E25 motorway for about 15 kilometres until signs for the centre of the city are encountered. Follow these into the city centre keeping an eye out

153

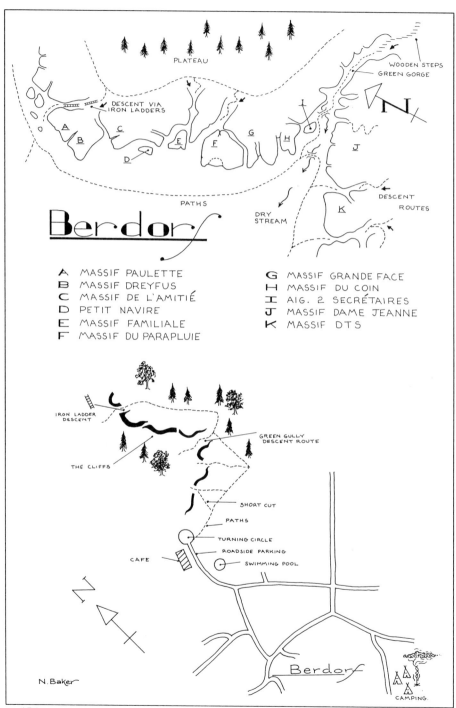

Berdorf

A MASSIF PAULETTE
B MASSIF DREYFUS
C MASSIF DE L'AMITIÉ
D PETIT NAVIRE
E MASSIF FAMILIALE
F MASSIF DU PARAPLUIE

G MASSIF GRANDE FACE
H MASSIF DU COIN
I AIG. 2 SECRÉTAIRES
J MASSIF DAME JEANNE
K MASSIF DTS

PLATEAU

WOODEN STEPS
GREEN GORGE

DESCENT VIA
IRON LADDERS

N

G
H
I
J

DESCENT
ROUTES

PATHS

DRY
STREAM

K

IRON LADDER
DESCENT

GREEN GULLY
DESCENT ROUTE

THE CLIFFS

SHORT CUT

PATHS

TURNING CIRCLE

CAFE

ROADSIDE PARKING

SWIMMING POOL

N

N.Baker

Berdorf

CAMPING.

154

for signs for the E29 and Echternach. Once located this road is followed out of the city through the towns of Junglinster and Graulinster until a minor left turn to Consdorf and Berdorf is reached about 25 kilometres from Luxembourg. This junction is easily overshot on the fast straight road. Drive through Consdorf on to Berdorf about 8 kilometres from the junction.

WHERE TO STAY
There are several exceptionally pleasant campsites in the small village of Berdorf and in the other towns scattered through the area. The facilities are invariably of the highest order and prices are very reasonable. The sites do get busy in the high season though it is uncommon to see them full. Booking in advance is a possibility and the address and phone numbers of several of the sites in Berdorf are given in the front of this guide. The owners of the campsites usually speak good English.

APPROACHES
At Berdorf the main climbing area is a horizontal five minute stroll from the roadside parking at the semi-openair swimming pool. A wayside cafe (popular with the local wasps) offers cheap snacks, and drinks both soft and alcoholic: a great place for stopping off at the end of the day. Go past the turning circle and follow the path rightwards into the woods. At the only fork take the gated left-hand track passing some impressive piles of logs. This leads past a series of stations on the Fitness Parcours which can be used as a warm up by the really keen. After 400 metres at exercise station number 4 a large open gully on the left leads (steep and slippery) to the right end of the main section of the cliff at the **MASSIF DE LA DTS**. For those who can not contain themselves and don't mind working through this section of the guide backwards this offers the quickest approach to the cliff. In reality it is better to continue for another 300 metres to where there is a sign for the École Escalade Wanterbaach and the path descends steps into a rocky gully. It weaves down this and passes through an amazingly verdant ravine to arrive in the centre of the cliff between the flat-faced **AIGUILLES DES DEUX SECRÉTAIRES** and its vague painted crocodile on the right (looking downhill) and the massively leaning wall of the **MASSIF DAME JEANNE** on the left.

An even more logical approach at least on first acquaintance is to continue along the cliff top path as it sweeps round in a long loop and eventually reaches a set of iron steps that apparently disappear into the bowels of the earth. At the base of these turn left to arrive at the edge of the Massif Paulette at the left extremity of the most continuous section of the cliff. The routes are described from here massif by massif always from left to right. If on first acquaintance things appear rather confusing, persevere and all will become clear, see the map.

The cliff consists of a series of (generally) south- and west-facing towers and buttresses riven by chimneys and gullies of varying dimensions from off-widths to grand canyons. The detailed layout of the towers is quite bewildering at first sight but a little time spent exploring should sort the geography of the place out adequately.

There are easy descents from most routes to be found by walking a short distance back into the trees to pick up one of the many deep gullies. The most important of these are marked on the map. There are very substantial belay rings above all the climbs. A specific request has been made that climbers avoid lowering off or abseiling from the many large trees on the cliff top. The sawing action of the rope cuts through the bark and eventually kills the trees. It also generates enough heat to scorch nylon ropes, so please either abseil from the rings or walk round, you know it makes sense. If you must use the trees a long extension sling to take the rope over the cliff edge and screw gate karabines are sensible ideas.

Recently many of the harder climbs have had lowering stations fitted just below the cliff edge thus removing the need to battle over the rounded cliff edge and to top out, unless of course you are in "summit mode".

THE CLIMBS

The first piece of rock of any significance is a fine clean west-facing wall. Towards the left side of the upper section of this wall is a prominent leaning crack which provides the upper pitch of the classical La Paulette, the whole wall is named after this climb:

MASSIF DE LA PAULETTE

The first two climbs are short technical exercises that end at the belay below the crackline.

Petite Paulette * 6a (HVS 5b) 50ft ◊

Start at the left edge of the wall and climb the slab until it is possible to traverse right past a crack and along a flange that runs out to join **La Paulette** which is then followed back leftwards to its stance. Lower off or attack the crack above if you suddenly feel heroic.

Le 31ième Anniversaire * 6a (E2 6a) 40ft ◊

Climb the wide crack at the left side of the wall and continue up the thin slab following the old cemented pegs (the new bolts just to the right appear to belong to a recent eliminate, clip them if you want) to the belay of **La Paulette.**

La Paulette *** (E2) 90ft

A fine varied climb up the highest part of the wall. Unless you are into off-widths it might be good idea to try and sandbag your mate into leading the top pitch! Start at a right facing yellow flake down the slope from the final crack.

1. 60ft   6a+ (5c) ◊ Climb the flake until it starts to run away to the right then pull leftwards over the roof to gain a groove. Continue trending up and left to reach a small stance below the ever widening crack in the leaning headwall.

2. 30ft   5 (5b)   The crack takes no prisoners, big fists and a determined approach help in the assault. If all else fails a frantic laybacking session might be the key!

The superb steep wall to the right of the start of **La Paulette** is tackled centrally by the big butch character of

Jacques *** 7b+ 80ft ◊

Follow the ramp line left of the deep chimney (cemented ring peg) then climb straight up to the roof. Cross this to reach a large pocket then storm on up the sustained and tough wall to the top. If the climb proves too tough you will just have to Jacques it in! Recently bolted eliminates to left and right are 7c and 7c+.

The cliff is now split by a deep rift, the first of many such fissures that fracture the cliff. (Climbers who love those desperate gritstone chimneys that are usually graded **Hard Diff** and are really **E2** will realise at this juncture that they have found paradise.) The rocks then swing round to face south and present a fine face rising above the trees and some rather incongruous tubular steel fencing that has been erected to cut down on the erosion that the base of the cliff is suffering from. This wall is home to several fine climbs and is known as the:

MASSIF DREYFUS

Several of the climbs here have their names painted on the rock at the foot of the routes (eco-vandalism or route finding without tears?) though many of these are very faded. The first route explores the chimney that separates the **MASSIF DREYFUS** from the **MASSIF PAULETTE**.

Chimney Dreyfus * 3 (Severe) 80ft

A classic of its kind (its kind being deep dank dark chimneys). Pass either side of the obligatory chockstone to a blinding exit back to the land of sweet smelling pine and sunshine.

The next climb is much more open, climbing the exposed edge of the chimney. It is reached by a rising traverse from around the right side of the arête and starts below the main section of face.

Dreyfus Normal *** 4 (Severe) 90ft

From ledges below the overhangs on the front face of the buttress shuffle leftwards past a yellow bolt in a position of rapidly increasing exposure. Once gained the arête gives pleasant climbing with big holds and great situations.

The steepest part of the face of the buttress has two classic routes each of which is marked by a line of cemented peg runners.

Franco-Lux ** 6a (E2 5c) 80ft ◊

Start from a block and ledges below the left side of the face and follow the left-hand line of cemented pegs slightly leftwards up the steepening rock until a short traverse left is possible to gain the upper crack system. This is sustained and tricky (no sneaking around left onto the previous climb) until a couple of moves back to the right gain the belays.

The yellow bolts between this and the next route is some glory seekers' idea of an eliminate, blinkers essential at 6b+.

Foquet-Duchesne *** 6b (E2 5b) 80ft ◊

A great route and a "reet pumper" with the crux right at the very top. Watch your pronunciation when people ask you what you are on!

From a left-facing corner follow the right-hand line of cemented pegs past a 6ft wide slot to ledges. Continue up a flake with increasing difficulty to a final thin sequence to the belays. The installation of the chains below the cliff edge means that there is no longer any need to do battle with the sloping holds and rounded rock that lead to cliff top just above, what a relief and what a cop out!

The shallow corner that bounds the right side of the steepest part of the face gives another classical pitch albeit at a more amenable grade.

Ecureuil *** 5+ (HVS 5a) 70ft

Follow the shallow left-facing corner until a couple of steeper moves are needed to get into the deeper right facing continuation. Scamper up this on good holds always keeping your eyes open for hidden hoards of nuts.

To the right of the groove line of **Ecureuil** is a flakey face that runs rightwards to end at a wide chimney, this contains four worthwhile though rather tightly packed pitches.

Edelweiss ** 5+ (HVS 5a) 70ft

Start at a roofed in corner to the right of the base of **Ecureuil** and climb up right before stepping left to reach a white niche. Follow the flake that springs from here to the cliff top. Bellowing out "the hills are alive with the sound of music" may just be acceptable on this climb if you can't remember the words of Edelweiss.

La Fête de Pères ** 5 (HVS 5a) 70ft

Begin on a ledge in a corner and climb up to join **Edelweiss** briefly just before it steps out left. From this juncture head away right up a flake that runs to the top of the wall.

Gentiane ** 5+ (HVS 5b) 70ft
Start as for the previous climb but ascend the shallow right-facing corner before crossing the left edge of a roof and following the continuation flake that goes to the cliff top.

L'Oglee * 5 (HVS 5a) 70ft
The right arête of the wall is followed throughout starting at the foot of the wide and very deep chimney crack that delineates the right edge of the wall. Pleasantly sustained.

Cheminée du Lezard * 3+ (Severe) 60ft
The chimney is really more of a caving trip than a climbing route, knee pads are a good idea though a head torch may be naughty; get grovelling.

To the right of the chimney the cliff juts forwards as a flaky wall (don't get excited, its not THE Flaky Wall) and has a large pointed block, **THE PETIT NAVIRE**, standing in front of its central section. This is the

MASSIF DE L'AMITIÉ
The routes on this buttress are quite short though they make up for a lack of stature by being action packed. The first climb is on the narrow west-facing wall of the buttress.

Bleusard ** 6b+ (E3 6a) 50ft ◊
The lower section of the face gives thin and fingery climbing, fortunately both the angle and the technical difficulties ease as height is gained. Finish up the slab.

Just around the arête to the right is a line of cemented pegs. These provide the protection on

Aspirant Moniteur ** 6b (E1 5b) 50ft
Follow the line of pegs steeply until a tricky couple of moves can be made to gain the slab on the left. This provides a contrasting delicate finish to the climb.

Véronique ** 6a (E2 5c) 50ft
Start 6ft right of the arête and follow a line of flakes steeply until is possible to scratch leftwards round onto the slab and relieve the straining on your arms. A touch of teetering remains to reach the top.

La Sans Nom ** 5+ (E3 5c) 50ft
An eliminate line up the centre of the wall (you don't need to tell me that the grades don't add up!). A prominent large flake is reached with difficulty and followed to rest on the right. Step back left then finish direct by thin sustained climbing past

159

a pair of rather decrepit pegs.

The next five climbs start behind the pointed block of the **PETIT NAVIRE** and are reached by a short scramble up a gully.

L'Amitié *** 6a (E2 5c) 50ft

A fine climb starting at the double flakes just to the left of the entry to the rift. Climb to the second peg runner then trend left to a niche. When suitably refreshed follow the flakes back to the right almost to the corner before swinging left into the steep finishing crack.

La Felyane ** 6a (E2 5c) 50ft

Start as for the previous route but continue the diagonal line of ascent to gain and finish up the final section of the main corner on the right.

Spinne ** 6b (E2 5c) 50ft

Follow the steep angular corner that bounds the right side of the wall throughout to finish steeply as for the previous climb.

Three feet right of the corner is;

V'ième Anniversaire *** 6a (E2 5b) 50ft

Getting your hands and feet over the roof is easy, getting your dangling backside over is less so. Once ensconced follow the crack to its apex then climb the leaning wall rightwards on a superb and continually surprising set of finger holds.

Pulling round the initial overhang on V'ième Aniversaire, 6a (E2 5b), MASSIF DE L'AMITIÉ, BERDORF.
Climber: Graham Parkes

Nearing the top of a sun dappled Tulipe 6b (E3 5c), MASSIF DE L'AMITIE, BERDORF. Climber: Nigel Baker

La Remoise ** 6c (E3 6a if you are 6' 3" though possible much harder for the altitudinally disadvantaged**) 40ft**
The centre of the wall to the right of the corner is severely undercut. Get established on this with difficulty (and knees) then make a couple of long reaches to easier rock.

The final three climbs on the **MASSIF DE L'AMITIÉ** are found where the cliff swings round to form a leaning wall rising to the right of the deep chimney/toilet at the "backside" of the **PETIT NAVIRE**. To avoid stepping in something unsavoury it is probably best to walk around the outside of the tower rather than squeeze through the smelly darkness at its "rear".

Yellow Submarine ** 6a+ (E2 5c) 60ft
Climb the "beatling" bubbly right arête of the toilet via a layback flake to reach steep sustained climbing on the upper wall.

Tulipe * 6b (E3 5c) 60ft**
The central line on the wall is a superb steep pitch, with a bulging start up a shallow groove and the expected jugs never quite materialising.

Teddy ** 6b (E3 6a) 60ft
'he right arête of the wall is a cuddly little number being both steep and a touch ₅andy. The crux involves a l-o-n-g reach from a layaway to a distant pocket. The

161

edge of the **MASSIF DE LA FAMILIALE**, lurks behind you, too far away to bridge to but probably close enough to hit if you muff the crux moves.

The next small collection of short routes is to be found on the large pointed block that stands in front of the **MASSIF DE L'AMITIÉ**. This is the

PETIT NAVIRE, and although diminutive there is at least the reward of what Americans always refer to as "a summit experience". The routes are described anti-clockwise starting at the top of the gully between the **MASSIF DE L'AMITIÉ** and the **PETIT NAVIRE**.

Escalier Amont 2 (Diff) 25ft

Just around the corner at the top of the gully this is the easiest way up to, and the usual way down from, the summit of the block.

Face Nord 4 (VS 4b) 25ft

The centre of the right wall of the gully.

Arête Ouest 4+ (VS 4c) 30ft

The sharp arête on the right as you enter the gully offers a few pleasant manoeuvres and is tackled on its right side.

The outer face of the block offers some longer and correspondingly more worthwhile pitches.

L'Oblique * 6b (E1 5c) 30ft

The steep front face of the block is climbed to gain a ramp, up this to a steep finish.

Poupe * 6a (E2 5c) 35ft

The right arête of the block starting behind the tree is followed throughout. Quite short but steep enough to ensure you get pouped!

To the right of the previous climb is the chimney/toilet mentioned earlier and then the steep wall with the last three routes on the **MASSIF DE L'AMITIÉ**. To the right of this is a gully and its right side is formed by the large tower of the **MASSIF DE LA FAMILIALE**. The recessed position of this piece of rock and a collection of lower grade routes means that it is a good place to pick if you want to have a quiet epic away from the prying eyes of those superior creatures who always appear at the most inopportune moments. The routes are described from left to right starting at the top of the gully on the left side of the buttress.

Familiale Directe 3+ (Severe) 30ft ◊

7m up the gully is a prominent steep crack leading to a flake up which the route finishes.

Familiale Normale * 2+ (Diff) 30ft ◊

The prominent left-rising ramp offers the easiest way up the tower, and is the normal descent. The peg at the top can be used to abseil from, or to back-rope the last man down.

Voie du Rétablissement * 5 (HVS 5a) 30ft ◊

From the foot of the ramp climb directly up the wall past a selection of nice new bolts. Just when you thought the route a pushover a thin move is required to reach the chains.

Arête de la Familiale * 4+ (VS 4c) 40ft ◊

Step out right to reach a ledge on the arête then follow it throughout to the chains on the crest of the wall.

The next two routes are found on the west face of the tower, the first one starting behind the holly tree.

Traversée Piene Perdu * 6a (E2 5c) 40ft

Climb leftwards up the wall until close to the arête then trend back right for a steep finish.

Pilier de la Familiale ** 3 (V.Diff) 40ft

The open groove at the right side of the west face gives a good pitch finishing up a wide crack that is fortunately easier than it appears from below.

The final climb on the buttress is found around to the right up the wide gully and starts 5m right of a boxed-in holly.

Traversée Ouest 4 (VS 4c) 40ft

Bridge up a wide chimney to a pedestal on the left then traverse left along a ledge system for 20ft to join and finish up the previous route.

Behind the **MASSIF DE LA FAMILIALE** there lurks the even more retiring **MASSIF DU GRAND PAS**. I have not described any routes on this particular buttress but if you enjoy exploring the place is worth a visit. On the right side of the gully that runs under the **MASSIF DE LA FAMILIALE** is the left end of the extensive **MASSIF DU PARAPLUIE**, a magnificent buttress and one of the most imposing on the cliff. It is short and relatively easy-angled at the back, opposite the routes just described. Around to the right there is the fiercely-leaning west-facing side wall that beetles above a gully containing a series of low stone walls. This imposing face has some atmospheric routes weaving their respective ways up it which feel much bigger that they appear from below. The left side of this can be identified by the spurious warning triangle (falling rocks) that is painted high up the wall. Finally the buttress swings round and towers over the path along the

Graham Parkes
approaching the
'danger zone' on
La Plage, 6a+ (E2
5c), Berdorf,

foot of the rocks
presenting some very
impressive over-
hangs.

The first routes
start at the top of the
gully on the right.

Cyrano ** 5 (VS 4c) 40ft

Start at an arête at
the left side of the
face where the
painted name is just
discernible. Traverse
right onto the face
and climb to a series
of roofs that are
skirted on the right to
reach easier climbing
and then the summit.

J.F. ** 5 (VS 4c) 50ft

Start where the face
swings round and
starts to lean steeply (name on the rock). Climb the steep wall and crack leftwards
to reach ledges on the previous route. Trend right from here up the wall to gain
a groove that leads to the cliff top.

La Plage *** 6a+ (E2 5c) 70ft ◊

A magnificent pitch, the first of several steep and rather harrowing classics. Start
at the large name on the rock and follow the discreet arrows (they indicate the line
and some of the more well hidden holds!) to pass the warning sign with difficulty.
Finish steeply to chains on the crest of the wall.

Lionel Terray *** 5+ (E1 5b) 80ft

Just to the right of **La Plage** is a steep crack. Climb this then swing right to reach further cracks that lead to a hollow and a rest. Move right then cross the bulges to gain a flake that is followed to the cliff top, superb.

25ième Anniversaire Direct *** 6a (E2 5b) 90ft ◊

Another storming trip up the centre of the wall that hangs over the gully. Start at a prominent steep jamming crack that leads to bulges, down the slope from the previous climb. At the bulges swing right to gain a rest below frowning overhangs. Here it is possible to regain some composure before taking a deep breath and going for it. The jugs keep appearing as long as you keep pulling, until eventually the angle eases at the foot of a large impressive slab. There are two ways up this, either the right line at 5b or the left line at precarious 5c, take your pick.

25ième Anniversaire *** 5+ (E1) 100ft

The original route of the wall gives a great outing with an atmosphere out of all proportion to its size, feeling more akin to the great classics of South Stack rather than some wooded outcrop climb. Start as for the **Direct**.

1. 60ft   5+ (5b)   Climb the jamming crack to the first new bolt then trend right following the obvious weakness to a bolt and peg belay in a niche.

2. 40ft   5 (5a)   Follow the steep twisting crack line above the stance to easier angled rock and the top of the tower, quite superb.

The next climb tackles the steeply bulging left arête of the front face of the buttress and loosely follows the original aid route that the buttress is named after. As you might expect from its title the main pitch of the climb can be done in any weather.

Parapluie *** 7a 70ft ◊

A steep and technical piece of climbing. Start just left of the arête and climb a series of corners to a large roof. Move right and pull through using a series of spaced pockets to reach much easier rock leading to the belay of the previous climb. Finish up this or lower off.

There appears to be another free route just to the right of the last climb whose name is a series of hieroglyphics, though I have been unable to come up with any details about the climb. It looks very good and pretty tough!

The front face of the **MASSIF DU PARAPLUIE** is the impressive west-facing wall with a broad band of overhangs at one third height, that towers over the footpath at the foot of the cliff. This is the scene of many old aid routes and has yet to be seriously invaded by devotees of the "modern approach". When it is addressed there will be some spectacular pitches here.

To the right of the **PARAPLUIE** a set of wooden steps leads up a massive tree

Nearlng the top of the wide crack on Grande Face 2, 5+ (E2 5b), MASSIF DE GRANDE FACE, BERDORF. Climber: Mike Appleton

and a huge black chimney above a mushroom-shaped block. This chimney is the **Cheminée de la Vache** and it runs right through the cliff separating the **MASSIF DU PARAPLUIE** from the **MASSIF DE LA GRANDE FACE**. The chimney can be climbed at a whole series of different depths mostly at about grade **4 (VS)**. Describing these is both difficult and perhaps a little pointless, though experiencing at least one of the ways out of the blackness is worthwhile. The fact that a couple of the exits are called **La "Spe"** and **La "Leo"** should give an indication what to expect. You may also come to realise where the name **Cheminée de la Vache** came from.

To the right of the chimney is the **MASSIF DE LA GRANDE FACE** which despite its name is not quite the tallest buttress at Berdorf. The upper section of the buttress is a fine slab, direct access to which is again guarded by some large overhangs. Fortunately there are a couple of ways through these, allowing scope for some mixing and matching of pitches. The first climb starts off the mushroom-shaped block and is

Grande Face 4 & Free Reality *** 6b (E3 5c) 90ft
From the fungus-shaped protuberance (mushroom-shaped block to you) climb the overhanging groove rightwards on to the slab and a possible belay at the foot of a diagonal crack. From here continue directly up the fine sustained slab above.

Grande Face 2 & La Guy *** 5+ (E2 5b) 90ft
Start at the name and climb the inset wall rightwards to gain the chimney crack in the centre of the buttress. Improvise your way up this to the possible stance of the previous climb, then step right and climb the centre of the upper slab with

sustained interest.

Grande Face 2 & L'Oblique ** 5+ (E1 5b)

A rather unbalanced climb with a claustrophobic lower section and much easier climbing above. Approach the hanging chimney of the previous route from directly below and swim up into it. Continue to the possible stance of the previous two climbs then follow the diagonal crack out to the left arête of the buttress 3+ (Hard Severe) and finish up this in a fine position.

To the right and just before the buttress swings round to face south is another fierce chimney line. This is

Grande Face 1 *** 5+ (E1 5b) 80ft

A "gob-smacking" line which gives a classic struggle with a possible stance at half height if you feel you have done enough thrashing for one day and want to give your mate a go.

The overhangs to the right of the chimney are reputedly breached by **La Sirène** at **7a**, though to be quite honest it looks unlikely at the grade.

The cliff now swings round to present a fine flat wall that faces south. The left arête of this is the impressive piece of rock dead ahead when you cross the footbridge westbound, and the ascent of this is much easier than appear-ances might otherwise indicate.

Miroir Gauche *** 6a (E1 5b) 80ft ◊

Trend left passing a large ring peg to get established on the arête. Follow it over a couple of bulges then trend back right to finish in the centre of the wall. If the start proves too much it is possible to climb further up the wall then trend left to the arête.

The steep lower section of Miroir Gauche, 6a (E1 5b), MASSIF DE GRAND FACE, BERDORF. Climber: Mike Appleton

Judd Mat Gardebounen * 7b 70ft ◊

The centre of the wall gives a pitch of escalating difficulty to the obvious smooth section of rock which is passed by a couple of desperate moves using a brace of pathetic drilled pockets. The upper section is much easier.

The right side of the face has a prominent crack rising steeply up to the right. Logically this is the

Fissure Oblique ** 4 (Hard Severe 4a) 70ft

Climb steeply to the crack and follow it rightwards into an easier finishing corner.

Across the gully is a fin-shaped tower to the right of a large pine tree. The buttress is further identified by a steep ramp in its right side. This is the **MASSIF DU COIN**. The first climb takes the corner at the top of the gully on the left side of the fin.

Coin * 4+ (VS 4c) 40ft

Toss for the lead perhaps? Start up the easy blocky corner to reach a scoop then continue up the steeper crack to the flat top of the tower.

Paul Bessier ** 4+ (VS 4c) 50ft

Climb the bubbly arête of the tower on generally good holds until it is possible to traverse round onto the left-hand face to a ledge. The steep wall above this is climbed to an easier finish.

Malou ** 6a+ (E2 5c) 50ft ◊

Start as for the previous climb but stay on the right-hand face to climb the sustained and precarious ramp line to the chains. Keep cool and keep padding.

Across the gully is the last buttress that is described on this side of the Wanterbaach. This is the **AIGUILLE DES DEUX SECRÉTAIRES**, and it is identifiable by the large but rather faded "Lacoste" crocodile painted on its front face. There are a small collection of good steep pitches here.

Grande Fissure * 4+ (VS 4c) 30ft

The steep and bubbly rift in the left wall of the tower gives a pleasantly aggressive piece of climbing.

Les Deux Secrétaires ** 6b (E3 6a) 40ft ◊

The left arête of the tower is approached by swinging in from the left and gives a sustained and fingery pitch, with the chains on the right at the top.

Danielle *** 7a 40ft ◊

Make snappy moves up the centre of the crocodile face via a shallow ramp, nicely technical and nicely safe!

Arête Droit *** 6b (E3 5c) 40ft ◊

The right arête of the tower is climbed on its left hand side to give another fine sustained pitch.

Sachenriss ** 5 (HVS 5a) 30ft

The steep crack behind the tree in the south face of the tower gives a classical exercise in jamming with the added attraction of bolt protection.

To the right is a selection of buttresses which are called the ROCHERS VERTS for obvious reasons. For equally obvious reasons no routes are described here. The next buttress to be described is the imposing **MASSIF DE LA DAME JEANNE** that towers over the footbridge across the embryo Wanterbaach. This is unquestionably the finest piece of rock at Berdorf and as would be expected contains a fabulous collection of climbs.

MASSIF DE LA DAME JEANNE

A huge piece of magnificent sandstone, up to 100 feet high and very steep throughout its length. The left side of the buttress overhangs acutely and has a superb groove line which is climbed by **Cima Ouest**. To the right the lower section of the wall is split by a hand crack than runs half way up the cliff then fizzles out, the line of **Tapis Roulant**. Right again is an impressive chimney then a huge smooth looking wall directly above the footbridge. This is home to the classic **Heinz** and **Willy** as well as some more recent additions. Right again a large slab, the **Plan Incliné** (with its small but conspicuous tree) hangs above an undercut wall and finally the buttress swings round to provide the smoothest piece of rock on the whole cliff, home to the legendary figure of **Herman Buhl**.

Cima Ouest *** 7c+ 90ft ◊

A stunning route utilising the grossly leaning groove that snakes its way up the left side of the buttress.

Climb a flake then the fine groove to horizontal jugs and a shake out. Head left up the indecently angled wall to big pockets above which more thin climbing gains a final groove and the chains. Lowering off gives an insight in to one of the reasons the climb is so hard (the other is the size of the holds!)

Tapis Roulant ** & 7b or *** & E2 5b with two bolts for aid 90ft ◊

Another great route up the centre of the wall. Unfortunately the short crux wall is much harder than the rest of the climb. Those who can do this section free will probably find the rest of the route rather too easy, whereas climbers operating at E2/3 can pull on a couple of bolts to produce a classic outing. The climb follows the prominent jamming crack in the centre of the wall and reaches this via a hanging slab below and left of the crack.

**The incredible
Cima Ouest, 7c+,
MASSIF DE LA
DAME JEANNE,
BERDORF**

Cross the slab and climb to the roof protected by a peg on the left (all quite problematical on first acquaintance) then traverse strenuously out right to a small ledge at the foot of the crack, possible stance. Jam the bulging fissure to its end then extemporize or aid your way up the "blank bit". Above this climb the steep wall on good holds and make a tricky move into the wide crack on the right. The chains are just a little higher in the right wall of the final wide crack.

Marylin *** 7a 80ft ◊

Another "stunner" up the wall between **Tapis Roulant** and the steep groove of the **Fissure Dame Jeanne** just to the right.

From below the deep groove climb the problematical wall leftwards until close to the possible stance on **Tapis Roulant**. Trend back right over the bulges before heading straight up the wall by long stretches for good holds to a short blank section which is passed using undercuts. Easier climbing then leads to a junction with the previous route which is followed to the chains. A good route for your first 7a, being both well protected and not too tough.

Fissure Dame Jeanne *** E2 80ft ◊

The deep overhanging groove to the left of the big chimney of Dame Jeanne with its in-situ tractor tyre gives a direct and atmospheric route.

1. 40ft   5+ (5b)   Bridge, layback and jam the fearsome inverted cleft until it is possible to swing out to reach rock of a saner angle and, just a little higher, a good stance.

2. 40ft   5+ (5b)   Follow the groove above the stance to where it is capped by bulges. Cross these steeply leftwards, the good holds keep appearing, until it is possible to sidestep leftwards to the belay of the previous routes.

Just right again is an impressive black chimney, just to the left of the footbridge and with a large (spare!) tyre hanging in its depths. This is climbed deviously by a low grade classic, well worth doing what ever league you operate in.

Dame Jeanne *** 4- (Severe) 90ft

1. 40ft   Head up the right wall of the chimney on good holds until it is possible to step across the other side and climb up to a finely situated stance on a prow.

2. 50ft   Follow the crack to the overhangs that block the way then traverse right to an exposed position on the arête of the chimney. Swing round the corner, then classical bridging up the cleft leads to the cliff top. If you find the exposure rather harrowing it is worth remembering that the further back into the cliff you head the darker it gets, that way you can't see the drop!

Dame Jeanne Directe ** 5- (HVS 5a) 80ft

The whole chimney can be climbed direct by an excellent varied pitch. The crux is the hanging narrows that the regular route neatly avoids.

To the right of the chimney is a superb scooped face that forms the right side of the **MASSIF DAME JEANNE**, rising directly above the footbridge and soaring above the trees. This fine wall is home to five routes, two superb older classics and three newer offerings. Amazing though it appears from the ground it is possible to do the routes and get back down on a single 50 metre rope.

Lutfikus ** 6b (E3 5c) 80ft ◊

The left arête of the wall is approached up easy rock until things begin to bulge. From here on the route is a bit of a gripper because of the angle of the rock and its slightly sandy nature, it is definitely a case of taking a deep breath and going like stink. Lowering back down is impressive as long as you dare open your eyes.

The left side of the face has two routes, these are Ishiki Alien 7b+ and Stop Perfo Bebe Dodo 7a+. They look at least as good as the routes further to the right, and so should be excellent. Right again are two more bolt lines, both established classics. There are several ways of reaching the ledge at the foot of the steeper section of the cliff and these can be used as short climbs at amenable grades if you don't really fancy the upward view from the ledge.

Willy *** 6c (E3 6a) 90ft ◊

Simply superb. Either climb the crack on the left side of the slab, **Poulette * 4 (VS 4c)** (don't chicken out) and move right to the ledge or climb to it directly from right behind the bridge * **(HVS 5a)**. From the bolt belays on the ledge step right and climb straight up the wall, sustained but generally on superb holds and perfect jams to a rest below the final section. This gives the crux and the main difficulty is sorting out which of the many chalked pockets are of any use; the question is willy flash it?

Heinz *** 6b+ (E3 6a) 90ft

A little less technical and slightly easier than its twin, though equally superb. Presumably named because there are 57 different ways of doing the crux sequence.

Start right of the bridge and climb through the overhangs to attain a crack and slab. Up this then out left to reach the edge of the ledge (possible belay on the left). Thus far the route is **Petites Vacances * 5+ (E1 5b)**. Climb rightwards through an area of softer rock to gain the face above. This gives more fine climbing generally on good holds and with the crux right at the very top (a Friend 2.5 might not go amiss if you don't fancy taking a spectacular back flip from the mantelshelf to gain the belay ledge).

Around to the right is a large hanging slab with a small but prominent pine tree growing out of it. This is climbed (the slab not the tree) by:

Plan Incliné *** 6a (HVS 5b) 90ft

A steep lower section gains the slab which is climbed leftwards to smoother rock which leads to small ledges and a possible stance. The even steeper crack above is gained from directly below (crux) and leads to the cliff top.

To the right is another impressive chimney crack, narrowing as it rises and

The superb upper section of Willy, 6c (E3 6a), MASSIF DE LA DAME JEANNE,
BERDORF. Climber: Graham Parkes

173

cutting through some impressive roofs. Fortunately the route is not the horrendous undertaking it first appears and it provides a low grade classic.

Dièdre *** 4+ (VS 4b) 80ft

Bridge the lower half of the rift, passing occasional peg runners to reach a ledge and possible belay on the left (4a). Step back right and continue up the rift, always imposing but never too difficult, to pop out suddenly on the cliff top.

The right arête of the chimney provides a steep and exhilarating climb for the talented.

Marguerite *** 7a 80ft ◊

Swing across the initial roof on "biffos" to gain the right side of the arête which is followed steeply and not always on good holds to even steeper rock. A couple of hard moves on well spaced and unhelpful holds should gain the chains.

A right-hand start is much harder:- 7b+.

The final wall of this massif lies around to the right, and is most impressive. The magnificent central line trending steadily rightwards up the smoothest section of cliff is **Herman Buhl *** 8a+ 80ft ◊**, enough said.

The lines to left and right are (I think) 7c and 6c.

The cliff is now split by a steep wide gully and beyond this is the last buttress: the imposing **MASSIF DE LA DTS** (Dalle - Toit - Surplomb, or slab, roof and overhang to the likes of you and me). The left side of this massif is a large rounded and rather green-looking buttress, the left side of which overlooks the wide gully. This side wall is climbed by a good route that initially starts on the front face at a large block below the overhangs.

Spigolo Giallo ** 6a (E1 5c) ◊

Swing right from the block to gain ledges then climb up and around to the left to reach the gully wall. Up this to bulges where a couple of tricky moves gain easier rock and the chains just below the cliff top.

Starting in the same place as **Spigolo Giallo** and heading up the front face of the buttress are two much tougher climbs.

Sump *** 7a 70ft ◊

Start as for the previous climb then climb the wall via sustained and "interesting" moves to gain a flake which leads to the chains. Excellent.

Le Infernal ** 7b 80ft ◊

A magnificent looking pitch that is unfortunately rather unbalanced with a couple of desperate moves on chipped holds at 60ft, with the rest of the climbing being much easier.

Swing right from the block under the left arête of the buttress then climb the wall rightwards on generally good though occasionally spaced holds to the "blank" bit. Levitate past this then continue more easily to the belays.

D.T.S. *** HVS 110ft

A classical route weaving a devious and interesting line up the centre of a very imposing buttress. Start in the centre of the buttress below the left edge of a slab that slants up to the right below the biggest overhangs.

1. 50ft 4+ (5a)   Climb over the initial roof to gain the foot of the slab then follow it up to the right by sustained and precarious moves by staying close to the roof. Steeper climbing leads up and right to gain a stance on the edge of the large chimney.

2. 60ft 4+ (5a)   Swing back left, very steep but on gigantic holds to gain a traverse line on the front of the buttress. Edge leftwards to gain the groove on the left edge of the buttress and finish up this with one tricky move just before the angle eases.

Directly above the start of D.T.S. is a gnarly-looking roof crack

Double Surplomb ** 7a 40/90ft

The roof crack is a classic of its kind: an unhelpful width, exhaustingly strenuous and sometimes green. All in all, great practice for **Harvest, Giggling Crack** or **Ramshaw Crack**.

The centre of the **D.T.S.** buttress is cleaved by another of the ferocious looking chimneys that Berdorf abounds with. This one is

Les Flammands *** 4 (VS 4b) 80ft

Climb the lower section of the route by classical chimney manoeuvres to a possible stance on the left. Step back right for the slightly more difficult upper section finishing left or right of the final block.

Right again is another large roof split by a curving thin hand crack that is often damp. This is the **Toit du Monde**, and although listed as an aid route in the last guide it looks like a contender for Luxembourg's answer to California's **Separate Reality**, any takers?

The final climb on the cliff lies around to the right where the beetling side wall of the gully is spilt by a slanting crack with a line of shiny bolts beside it.

Le Diable *** 7b+ 50ft ◊

A suitably demonic pitch for the final one on the cliff. Climb left across the initial roof then head up the leaning wall on crozzly holds to the final band of roofs that are tackled on slopers, pumpy in the extreme!

mountain / sports incorporating 'Mountain INFO'

Britain's liveliest and most authorative magazine for mountaineers, climbers and ambitious hillwalkers. Gives news and commentary from the UK and worldwide, backed up by exciting features and superb colour photography.

OFFICIAL MAGAZINE

Have you read it yet?

Available monthly from your newsagent or specialist gear shop.

Call 0533 460722 for details

BRITISH MOUNTAINEERING COUNCIL

IF YOU LIKE ADVENTUROUS ACTIVITIES ON MOUNTAINS OR HILLS YOU WILL ENJOY

CLIMBER

& HILLWALKER

MOUNTAINEERING/HILLWALKING/TREKKING ROCK CLIMBING/SCRAMBLING IN BRITAIN AND ABROAD

AVAILABLE FROM NEWSAGENTS, OUTDOOR EQUIPMENT SHOPS, OR BY SUBSCRIPTION (6-12 MONTHS) FROM CALEDONIAN MAGAZINES LTD, PLAZA TOWER, EAST KILBRIDE, GLASGOW G74 1LW